HOW MANY LABELS DOES ONE CHILD NEED?

TARA MARDIAN (MOTHER)

Copyright © 2020 Tara Mardian

Formatting by Indie Publishing Group

ISBN: 978-1-7772301-0-4 Paperback
ISBN: 978-1-7772301-1-1 Hardcover

All rights reserved, including the right to reproduce this book or portions thereof in any form whatsoever. Apart from any fair dealing for the purpose of research, private study, criticism or review, no part of this publication may be reproduced, stored in or introduced into a retrieval system, or transmitted in any form or by any means (electronic, mechanical, photocopying, recording or otherwise), without the prior written permission of the copyright owner. When the author wrote this version of her story she wrote from a place of love for all of the mentioned individuals in, so some names and identifying details have been changed to protect the privacy of those individuals. It is written from the perspective of the author, and the author alone. There is no doubt, there are not other perspectives, but this is a mother's voice. The information provided in this book is designed to provide helpful information on the subjects discussed. This book is not meant to be used, nor should it be used, to diagnose or treat any medical condition. For diagnosis or treatment of any medical problem, consult a physician, specialist or spiritual advisor. The author is not responsible for any specific health or allergy needs that may require medical supervision and are not liable for any damages or negative consequences from any treatment, action, application or preparation, to any person reading or following the information in this book. References are provided for informational purposes only and do not constitute endorsement of any websites or other sources. Readers should be aware that the websites listed in this book may change.

DEDICATION

There are way too many people that I could thank for being with me on this journey in life and you know who are you. My words could never express to all of you what you have meant for me, but I hope your hearts know. I also don't want to name everyone because I would likely accidently miss naming someone. There are people out there who we have only had minimal encounters with who make huge impacts on us every single day, so I'm sending light and love to everyone in my life. You are all a part of what makes me ...me. I want to honourably mention those who assisted with the actual support in creating this piece. Angela if it wasn't for you being my accountability partner, I would have never made it through to the end. You have been with me the entire way, so this creation was created because you held my hand. Thank you. Heather, thank you for helping to clear a pathway when I was creating personal blocks within myself, I would have never pushed through in finishing my story if it wasn't for you checking in with my guides and the records for knowing when it was ready. Michelle, thank you for being my peer reviewer, which allowed me to be vulnerable in sharing my story for the first time. Erminia and Gina Fusarelli aka "The Twins", thank you for being such powerful psychics who assisted me through spirit in naming and birthing this book. Moreover, most importantly thank you to my son and my daughter both for choosing me as your mom. I love you more than you love me, and yes anything is possible.

CONTENTS

Prologue vii

Part One - Game On 1
Chapter 1 - How It Started 3
Chapter 2 - The Beginning 9
Chapter 3 - The Judgement 13
Chapter 4 - Comparisons 19
Chapter 5 - The Obligation 23
Chapter 6 - Perspectives 27
Chapter 7 - Incidents 33
Chapter 8 - Unpredictable 39
Chapter 9 - A New Beginning 47
Chapter 10 - Defining Moment 51
Chapter 11 - Finally 57
Chapter 12 - Trial And Error 61
Chapter 13 - Marriage 65
Chapter 14 - Frustration 69
Chapter 15 - Exhausted 73
Chapter 16 - The Dark Side 77
Chapter 17 - Brain Waves 81
Chapter 18 - A Way Out 83
Chapter 19 - False Acceptance 87
Chapter 20 - It's Time 91

Part Two - Checkmate 97
Chapter 21 - Following My Instincts 99

Chapter 22 - Ticks And Tokens. 103
Chapter 23 - Statistic 107
Chapter 24 - Alternative Measures 111
Chapter 25 - The Truth. 113
Chapter 26 - Create Space 119
Chapter 27 - Higher Purpose 123
Chapter 28 - New Lens. 127
Chapter 29 - Balance 133
Chapter 30 - A Knowing. 137
Chapter 31 - Saviour. 141
Chapter 32 - Adapting 145
Chapter 33 - Now What. 149

Reference List **151**

PROLOGUE

I WATCH ANXIOUSLY, FROM across the room, my seven-year-old son, Scott, contemplate a newborn baby girl who's quietly sleeping. She is nestled in her car seat, at the entryway of our new home. Scott slowly lifts his arm and points his loaded Elite Raptor Strike Nerf gun directly at the baby's head. In that split second before he shoots, he looks over at me and locks eyes with mine. I recognize that look; it is one I have seen many times. He understands exactly what he is about to do, and wants me to know that he is going to enjoy every moment of that baby's cries. I have no time to react.....in that split second, I realize I have been playing chess with a mastermind. The mother, Sara in the midst of her taking off her coat sees what he is about to do. She stops what she is doing and runs to try to stop him… but the gun goes off. She didn't have a chance. Sara falls to her knees, sobbing hysterically, and before I can even apologize she leaves… without even saying goodbye. That was the last time we ever saw Sara and her baby girl.

I had just met the mother, Sara, last week when we moved into this small city after my husband Jack and I officially decided not to live together anymore. I met her when I was at the local Yoga Studio; we were both enrolling in the same class. I thought it was time to make friends, so I invited her back to my place for a coffee and a play-date. I never once thought that Scott would hurt her newborn baby girl..

I had no way of actually knowing which part of Scott's brain was taking over. I was never quite sure if it was anxiety or control. My heart wanted to believe he was a sweet little boy who wasn't in control of himself ... until that glare in his eyes revealed an aspect of him having a focused intent to cause harm that sent shivers down my spine. Scott did whatever Scott wanted to do. He was always the one in control.

I learned quickly that Scott needed to know that if I said I was going to do something, I had to follow through. If I showed him any bit of weakness, he would continue to test me in every way he could. In every moment I had to find a way to regain control; he could not be in control of me and our home.

I had to make a move…… and fast! Two days later, I made a rule that Scott was only allowed to shoot people if they had a weapon in their hands, or I would throw his Nerf guns out. I explained that it wasn't a fair fight to attack an innocent person. He told me that he understood. I made the consequences clear. Right before bed that night I was in the kitchen making myself a cup or tea when Scott stealthily approached me with his Nerf gun in hand, he gave me the satisfactory kill look, and shot me point blank in the head. I grabbed his gun and threw it in the garbage. He was so mad that he went to his room, screaming and kicked the door. He came out of his room with a vengeance, grabbed the Nerf gun out of the garbage, gave me a smirk, a threatening look, and said, "What are you going to do about it, Mom?"

He appeared to be loving this. So, I knew my next move had to be big in order for him to consider me a serious player in his game. I grabbed the gun from his hands and smashed it over my knee. I threw the two halves in the garbage. My knee was throbbing, but there was no way I could show weakness at this moment.

His face expressed a state of shock, and he instantly ran out the front door and down the street into the dark. I was devastated. What had I done? It was eight o'clock at night and my younger daughter, Layla was sleeping in her room, and I could not leave her to run after Scott, but I could not let him potentially run to his peril either. I left the house. I ran into the street yelling for him to come back. As I turned the corner, I saw him running down the middle of the street toward the main highway. I knew I could not run as fast as he could, so I just stood still and kept screaming, pleading for him to come back. Finally, in my desperation, I made a move that was a complete gamechanger. I yelled at the top of my lungs down our quiet street, "SCOTT, IF YOU DON'T GET BACK HERE RIGHT THIS INSTANT, I AM GOING TO THROW ALL OF YOUR POKEMONS IN THE GARBAGE!" He instantly stopped. He had been in complete control of his actions and the entire situation. What he had not expected was for me to start playing the game. He simply stared at me, so I yelled, "Ok you're not coming so I'm going to do it." I started to head back to the house. He ran fast to catch up with me. "Please mom, no mom, please don't throw out my Pokemon cards…MOM can you hear me, why aren't you listening to me, please mom NO." "OKAY!" I responded. "I won't throw them away this time. But if you run away like that or don't listen to the rules again, I'll do it, no question. Understand?" "I understand mom" he replied obediently.

I made a mental note of what I'd said because I would have to keep my threat. I was in control again. But honestly, I was never more terrified: I had no idea what to do or how to do it. Tomorrow would only bring another challenge and another move on the chess board that was our relationship. It was a game he seemed to instinctively be a master of and one I was only beginning to learn.

It was in these moments I would consider my dad's advice to be tougher with my son; but, how much tougher could I be? My mom thinks there is nothing wrong with her precious grandson. Scott's father says, "he'll grow out of it." Most people I encounter believe Scott is a nice well-behaved boy and that I'm too tough on him. *Am I too tough or too soft on him? What's wrong with me? Why can NO ONE see how difficult this truly is?*

My son has street smarts and is able to manipulate people without them knowing; but I knew … and he knew I knew. Then, out of the blue, he would have moments of complete weakness and his eyes would let me know how fragile he was. Those moments made me question whether what he did was intentional or not. So many questions, so much to figure out. But, ready or not, the game had started without me knowing I was even playing. It was GAME ON.

PART ONE
GAME ON

CHAPTER 1

HOW IT STARTED

AT TWENTY-SIX YEARS old, I was newly married and ready to be a mom. I'd wanted to be a mom since the age of sixteen. Even though I was university educated and had a career, I knew in my heart that being a wife and a mom would fill me with the most satisfaction. I had taken my education in Correctional services, but after college I went back home to Saskatchewan to figure out my life. My stepdad and mom helped me out by giving me a job on our family farm while I also worked at the local small town pub. That is where I met my soon to be husband Jack. He was very persistent in wanting to date me. He was a police officer and I always only saw him in uniform. The day he asked me out in his civilian clothing, I said yes. We were only dating for four months when he asked me to move to a nearby city with him because he got his dream job in that area. I said yes and I got a job in Social Services. We moved very quickly in our relationship and five months in a new place I said yes when he asked me to marry him. I thought that we would have lots of time before we settled down, but only a month after being married and I got the news that I was pregnant. Like any new mother, I was excited and nervous about the news since I had made all the right moves: I got my education before getting married—check; I got married before getting pregnant—check; I quit smoking before getting pregnant—check; I read all of the books on healthy pregnancies—check. I felt more than ready when the day finally arrived. Except, no birth ever goes as planned.

After my water broke, the doctor induced labour in order to reduce the risk of infection. But my baby was not ready to come into the world. It wasn't until twenty-five hours later that they instructed me to push because the risk to the baby was increasing with every passing hour. Most of that time is a blur. I vaguely remember pushing and holding, pushing and holding and, after five hours of that, the birth was no further along.

The doctor asked me if I still wanted him to use forceps or if I wanted a c-section. I could barely keep my eyes open and my body was trembling. I thought for sure I had done so much pushing that extensive damage to my body had already been done. No one told me that we were nowhere near the end of it. If I had known that at the time, I would have definitely opted for a c-section. But, I didn't; I chose forceps. After the third try to pull the baby out, I heard the nurses say we had gone too far. I was falling asleep and not able to continue pushing. The doctor refused to give up and I gave it one last try. Finally, ready or not, Scott was forcefully pulled into the world. Jack and I cried when we saw that beautiful little boy. In that moment Scott was perfect... our life was perfect.

My mom was there waiting to welcome Scott into the world. Even though I was exhausted, everything was blissful in those first few hours after his birth; Jack and my mom were there to cherish it all with me. We had other visitors and it wasn't until the day after when I was just waking up on the hospital bed to see my dad, grandma and step-mom there. They all had concerned looks on their faces and my dad said, "Tara, something isn't right. Your face is getting bigger." I noticed that even though my eyes were open I couldn't see the entire room. I thought it was just because I was just waking up, but when I moved the blanket off of my legs to get up and I looked down I saw my knee caps were no longer visible because my legs had doubled in size. I got up to look in the bathroom mirror and my entire face was ballooning up along with my entire body. My dad called the nurses. When the nurses arrived, they also looked worried and they called the doctor. Mom and Jack were back in the room with me when the doctor took one look at me and then ushered the whole medical team out of the room. I was worried and so was my mom, dad, step mom, grandma and Jack; I could see the worry on their faces. *What was happening?* When the doctor came back, he said I had pushed so long that all the blood vessels in my body had exploded, but they would eventually return to normal and the swelling would go down. What a relief it was to hear that it was only temporary. I felt traumatized by the labour and the fact that a doctor would let me push that hard and for that long. My parents also shared that they were worried the doctor had let it go on that far. I didn't know any different since it was my first time giving birth. Years later, I heard that the doctor had lost his medical licence. I couldn't believe it when I heard it, but maybe my labour story wasn't a normal one if he had lost his licence. I never heard why he lost his licence, but he only had pregnant patients. Regardless, as long as Scott was healthy and happy, that was all that mattered.

I thought things were going well, but we had already been in the hospital now for three nights. I initially thought we were in there longer because they wanted to monitor my body going back to normal. I was finally starting to be able to see my knee caps again when I noticed that Scott's skin was a lot more yellow than it had been previously. He was sleeping all the time and the nurse called him a "lazy nurser" because he fell asleep the second he latched onto the breast. Just when I thought we were getting closer to going home I was informed that we were not able to leave the hospital until the nursing staff was satisfied that he was eating well. I agreed completely because I wanted the additional support to figure out how to get him to eat.

I met three different nurses every single day because of shift changes. What I didn't expect was that ALL of the nurses had different advice. It wasn't that they were just offering different techniques, they made sure I knew they thought the previous advice I had received was wrong. I was told to pinch him; I was told to put a cold cloth on his head to wake him up in order to eat. It got to the point where I would tell the nurses to try whatever they thought would work because nothing was working for me. Scott just kept falling asleep the second he latched onto my breast.

The third night in the hospital, I finally broke down in tears and said I was done hurting him in order to get him to eat. The first few days of life shouldn't be this way. I pleaded with the nurses to give him formula. The nurses made me feel like I was giving up, like I was already a failure as a new mom. I felt completely defeated and judged. I was exhausted, and still trying everything they said over and over again.

The next night, when I was starting to get frustrated with trying to get Scott to latch on once again, an older night-shift nurse whom I hadn't yet met, came into my room. She watched me try a few times and then left the room. Shortly thereafter, she came back with a small bottle of formula and said, "Here you go, dear, I think you guys have been through enough."

She taught me a technique. If I pushed right under his

chin, a natural reflex occurs that causes him to suck in. She said there would be more difficult days, but that it would help us through the tough times. And even though I needed to force his chin to suck on the nipple of the bottle, I was no longer forcing him to wake up. I never felt so relieved in my entire life. I felt like I had been silently screaming inside from having one nurse after another tell me the nurse before her had told me the wrong thing.

When the morning shift came on, I was instantly criticized for using formula. I quickly learned to just tell the nurses that Scott was drinking from my breast, even though he wasn't. I fed him when there were no nurses present. They believed me so decided to release us. I was exhausted but relieved, overjoyed to be going home with my newborn baby. The worst was over. Or so I thought.

CHAPTER 2
THE BEGINNING

WHEN WE GOT home, things ran pretty smoothly for the first little bit. Until one day when Scott was about three months old and forcing the area under his chin to eat was no longer working. He would just fall asleep despite me forcing his reflux. Now instead, he cried all night. Being a first-time mom, I was lacking in confidence, because I just didn't know what I was doing.

I remembered what one of the nurses had tried; I resorted to trying her unorthodox technique. I stripped Scott's clothes off and laid his little naked body on the cold floor until he screamed. It was terrible… helplessly watching my baby go from a cry to a scream while I waited for the moment when he would start choking on air so I could feed him. If I gave in before that precise moment, he would fall asleep the second the nipple of the bottle hit his mouth. The third time I tried the technique, I broke down into uncontrollable sobs on the kitchen floor. Even though it was completely against my maternal instincts, I followed exactly what the nurses had told me to do because I thought they knew.

I realized in my desperate moments that there was no one who could help me. Because no one knew the answers. Everything about this baby seemed like nothing anyone could even relate to. He would sleep all day and cry all night. Everyone said ... he would eat when he was hungry. The problem was... he was never hungry. Now what? I just had to wait it out. I looked forward to when he could eat solid foods because I thought for sure feeding him would get easier as he got older.

It was my turn to learn the rules of the game and begin learning about my son. I pushed through those difficult days and just kept forcing him to eat, waiting for the next developmental stage. I did everything in opposition to what public health visitors told me to do. I put formula in his bottle even though they told me not to. I followed the advice of my mother instead of the health system. The nurses had told me to lay him on his back to sleep so he didn't suffocate while laying on his stomach. Little Scotty would fall asleep when he was on his tummy though. It was easier for Scott and me to figure out our own routine without the "officials" getting in the way. I was two steps ahead of them; I learned to tell them what they wanted to hear. Their statistics would falsely show that the advice they handed out worked.

It was starting to feel like I was getting the groove down when, finally, at six months of age, Scott started eating better. Man, did he love his solid foods. Night-times were SO much better. He slept well and was growing into an amazing little being. He loved to separate and coordinate anything with similar colours and shapes and he spent a lot of time repeating certain things over and over again. But, most importantly,... I noticed that his eyes never locked with mine. He would look at me, but he looked through me. I could never tell anyone that I didn't feel love or that building a bond with him took work.

The Beginning

A mother is supposed to completely and unconditionally love her child—right? I encouraged him and talked to him like any other mother did, but it was forced from me because it never felt like he truly looked at me. He was always hyper-focused on other things. I thought that once he got older, and we could play more together, it would be different. So, when he was eight months old, I went back to work and Scott went to daycare. This was when I realized, more than ever, that he and I were not connected at all. It took him going to a completely different environment for me to truly see the disconnect and differences between him and his peers. I was so embarrassed at how I felt that I never shared it with Jack or any of my friends or family. I kept all of my thoughts to myself hoping it would naturally get better.

CHAPTER 3

THE JUDGEMENT

JACK AND I worked out that it was easier for me to drop off and pick up Scotty everyday because Jack worked out of town most days. I was excited to go back to work, and all day I would have to interview kids on their home lives and how their parents treated them. It made me thankful that my son didn't have to grow up in an environment like some of those children were exposed to. I didn't have the best childhood, but I was committed that Scott would have a better experience than I'd had or any of the children the community were concerned enough about to call Child Protection about. Every day when I left work and headed over to his daycare, I felt an immense amount of gratitude for how good our life truly was. But, every single day, I was let down.

I realized quickly that I was the only parent whose child did not get excited when they saw them. My son would be fixated on going up and down the slide over and over again and not even respond to my voice when I called him. Even when I went right up to him, he wouldn't react when he saw my face. He showed no emotion towards me at all, no emotional expression either way. He would just continue in his current obsession. My heart would break every time. I had to hold back the tears when the staff would look at me with confused looks on their faces as to why my son wasn't excited to see me. I assumed that they thought there was something wrong with me as a mom. It would take ten minutes of immersion in his activity before he would realize I was even there and then, and only then, would I be able to take him away from that activity.

He didn't like hugs, so there was no rush to give me a hug; when I would try to give him one, he would pull away. He was driven by a motor and having to stop to embrace me wasn't an option. He was in control of our relationship. I had to wait to see what he was focused on before deciding what my next move would be. Nothing felt natural or fluid. Even when we would go home and watch a short show before bed, I would have to force myself beside him into his space in order to give him a hug. He would squirm when I held him, but I would hold him tighter and tighter until he relaxed and accepted my hug. He hated me touching him or even sitting beside him. It still brings tears to my eyes just to think about those times. I felt like I was in a constant state of trying to meet my own selfish need to connect with my son. Most children at this age have to be in close proximity to their parents or they get scared. It's because they have a healthy strong attachment. Scott never seemed afraid to be away from me… ever. In fact, he ran away from me all the time.

As soon as Scott learned to walk, he ran. He was always running. Grocery shopping with him was next to impossible. He would either run or have a meltdown in the cart. One time he climbed out of the cart when I was choosing apples and ran away. He didn't come back. I ditched my cart and ran all over the store searching for him. It was a split second and he was

The Judgement

gone. My heart stopped and a sinking feeling took over me. My knees just about collapsed when I heard over the intercom: "Is anyone missing a little boy?" Instantly relieved, I headed to the customer service desk. Scott was there, looking a bit scared, but calm. He was standing still, waiting patiently with the staff member. I was so embarrassed. I'm sure I appeared neglectful.

I needed a solution to my son's escapes. So, when I heard there were sneakers that squeaked for every step a child made, I was excited. They were supposed to motivate children to keep walking in order to hear their steps. I thought, *maybe, just maybe I will be able to hear if he runs away and know where he is going.* I carried Scott into a local store that sold the sneakers. As I put him down to pick up the shoes, he was gone in a flash. I turned around just in time to see him bolt out the door into the busy parking lot. My heart dropped and so did the shoe from my hand. I ran after him and caught up just in time; a vehicle was coming. They honked just as I grabbed his little body. I sat in my car and cried.... *How would I ever go out in public with him? I almost killed him.*

I could no longer operate like this; not only was I losing him, I was constantly checking the locks on the doors at home, paranoid that I may have forgot to lock it and he would run out of the house. So just before Scott turned three, I bought a good quality child's leash—the ones made specifically for children with disabilities. Finally, I felt free. Scott laughed that he was pulling me and that the faster he went the faster I went while I held the leash. He loved that he had the control over me and we started to have fun together with the leash. I was no longer sweating through my shirts just keeping up with him. I had him convinced it was a fun thing for him. He loved it. And I had control over the situation. I was free and so was Scott.

One day I was walking down the street and someone in the

distance yelled at me, "Are you going to teach him how to bark next?" I was devastated. That person had no idea that the leash was a safety measure. Scott would have been in the middle of the road, or gone, if I didn't have him tethered. I contemplated wearing a sign to explain his high energy. Everywhere we went, everyone would glare. People are quick to judge what they don't understand. Which was the lesser of two evils?: Keep Scott safe and make life easier for us or minimize our community exposure and criticism. I decided to ignore the judgment and keep using the leash. Safety first. The leash became our normal and I felt more confident about taking Scott for outings and experiencing new things together.

My husband suggested we go to West Edmonton Mall to play a round of mini golf. He thought Scott would love mini golf, and I would love to spend some time with my husband now that I was feeling a little less stressed. I told Jack the only way I was going was if Scott was on the leash. He didn't seem to mind, but he'd never really experienced using it, so he didn't have much exposure to the judgment it provoked. I didn't prepare him well enough for what we were about to encounter.

It was good at first. My husband could see that Scott would basically run on the spot while he was in front of me. He loved it. It wasn't until we got into the middle of the crowded mall that the judgment was unavoidable. Person after person passing us glared at us with disgust. I couldn't handle it. I unclipped the leash and held Scott in my arms. He screamed and wiggled right out of my arms. I caught him just in time before he took off. I instantly clipped him back to the leash. There was no way I was going to risk losing him in a big mall. I had to soldier on and ignore the looks, but my husband couldn't handle it. He looked at me with concern and said, "I'm sorry, I can't do this," and he walked ahead of me instead of beside me. My heart broke. I understood how he felt, but who else was going to do it? I would have to do it alone.

Scott had no idea about the conflict between his parents; he just kept laughing and yelling, "Hey, Mom, I'm pulling you, I'm pulling you." Glare after glare I pressed on until we were finally back at our vehicle. Jack and I did not even exchange words about it the entire two-hour drive back home. That was the last day I used the leash. I resorted to keeping Scott at home more and taking him out in public less.

Jack would always say.

"Scotty is a busy boy, but boys are busy and he will eventually grow out of it."

"Maybe you just need to take him outside more often to burn off his energy."

I worked so hard and sweat so much holding Scott or chasing him that I didn't need to go to the gym when we would venture outside. I believed parenting was generally just this hard. I had nothing to compare it to. Nevertheless, I couldn't handle it anymore.

I started to question myself. *Maybe Scott is fine, maybe it's just me. I'm the one who wanted the leash. Maybe he doesn't need it and it's the way I'm parenting him that makes him run.* I decided to look at how other moms with boys Scott's age were parenting and figure out what I was doing wrong.

CHAPTER 4

COMPARISONS

MOST MOTHERS OF my generation are called helicopter moms. Helicopter moms are the moms that hover over their kids to the point where they are never able to try things themselves, fall, experience any heartache, or have to problem solve themselves. I was not one of these moms. I am a loving, kind but strict, mom. I thought that was the way to parent. But why, oh why, was my child different than others? I even had playdates at the homes of friends who had boys, and noticed they could still have breakables out. I was shocked! How had their child not broken those yet? Of course, when we went to visit I was exhausted from chasing my son around their homes so he didn't touch their stuff and potentially break it. Even though I wasn't a helicopter mom, I had to hover over Scott everywhere we went to keep him safe.

My friend had twin boys the same age as Scott. Within thirty minutes of being in their home, he'd broken a vase. My friend said, "Hmmm... I never even considered that would be a hazard with my own boys."

Everything is a potential hazard with Scott. What stood out

How Many Labels Does One Child Need?

the most from those visits was the reaction her boys had when she disciplined them. They would cry if she told them "no" or slapped their hand. I almost cried the moment I realized this was a normal reaction to punishment. I have been normalizing all of Scott's reactions, and they weren't "normal."

A flashback replayed in my head of a time when I was cooking and I heard something smash in the living room. Scott was standing by one of my candles that he'd obviously just broken. I said "no" and slapped his hand. Nothing. No reaction at all. It was like I hadn't even slapped his hand. So, I just said "no" again and cleaned it up. Then, as I was walking away, he pushed my other candle over while looking straight at me. I couldn't believe he had done it. So, I gave him a spanking over his diaper and jeans hard enough to know it should have hurt. He looked mad and punched me. I stopped in my tracks. Mentally going through all of the things my parents taught me, I thought, *Wow, that must be why my generation says it's not good to spank, because it doesn't work.*

Searching through my minimal toolbelt for parenting tools, I gave him a time-out. *This should work,* I thought. The second I closed the door to his room, he ran out. I had no idea what I was doing wrong. I had to make sure to follow through with a consequence, so instead I held him on a chair while he screamed for the same amount of minutes for the age he was. I had learned that time-outs were supposed to be a minute per the age of the child. So, because he never stayed in the time-out I had to hold him for three minutes since he was three years old. It was the longest three minutes of my life. I was exhausted and confused about what I was supposed to do next time.

Fast forward to the present as I'm watching my friends' children having extreme emotional reactions to having their hands slapped. I wondered in that moment if it was my son who wasn't normal or my friends' boys who weren't normal. *Or, is it me who's not normal? I'm lost because you make parenting two look so much easier than my parenting one. What's wrong with me?* It kept repeating in my head: *What's wrong with me?*

If I've learned anything from being a social worker, it's that the child is never at fault. A parent needs to look at their own behaviour and change it. I need to do more investigating into the thoughts and observations my husband, and our families, had about Scott. Maybe there was something there. Maybe something genetic. Maybe it truly was just me. Maybe I wasn't meant to be a mom.

CHAPTER 5

THE OBLIGATION

WHEN WE WERE invited to birthday parties or playdates, I would tell Jack how nervous it made me because we would, undoubtedly, have to take Scott out of the place screaming by the end of it. It didn't matter how many strategies we were offered, none of them ever worked. Jack would always say, "Oh, he will be fine." But he wouldn't be. It made me feel like I was the only one who saw what was happening. I prevented social meltdowns by cancelling or being with Scott the entire time so that he could keep his focus on me alone. That strategy didn't work even if I told myself it did.

One day, out of total exhaustion, I screamed at Scott, "When Mom and Dad say it's time to go, IT'S TIME TO GO. GOT IT?" And it worked. We learned that he needed to be informed before we were at the party of the mere fact that we would eventually leave the party, so that he would know it would end when we said it would end. That was all he needed in order to stop what he was doing. It worked every single time after that. It calmed Scott down when he knew the plan, every single step of the way. I no longer planned things in my head; I said ALL of my thoughts aloud from then on so Scott felt fully informed on a daily basis. It was something no one ever told us to try; and it worked.

We went to Saskatchewan to visit my parents for Remembrance Day long weekend. Jack and my dad wanted us all to go to the ceremony at the Catholic Church.

Scott could not yet stay still, so I pleaded with Jack, "Please, Jack, Can Scott and I please stay home instead of going to the ceremony. You know that Scott won't be able to sit through that."

"He will be fine," Jack said.

Frustrated, I responded, "Yah, it will be fine because I'll make sure its fine because I have to do so much work to make it all work!"

Jack raised his eyebrow at me and repeated in a stern voice "It will be fine Tara!"

Jack never saw how much work raising our son truly was. My stepmom who heard the conversation looked at me with compassion. She gave me a long hug that almost made me cry. I felt like she understood me, yet couldn't help.

On our way to the church I knew I was going to have to entertain Scott. I held him on my lap during the service and rubbed his upper body repeatedly and played cars with him at the same time. I acted like a human chair in order to keep him contained and occupied. When it came time to stand up, my husband looked at me with disgust and said, "Why are you still sitting?"

I knew at that moment that if I interrupted what I was doing, Scott would stand up and, the second his feet hit the floor, he would want to start moving or running. My dad and Jack gave me "the look."—the one that says you're being disrespectful if you don't stand up. Therefore, I got up and Scott

The Obligation

started to run. I had to grab him fast and quietly try to engage him in playing with his cars again while attempting to convince him to get back to our seats. I was sweating profusely and was exhausted. I got him back just in time to end the service.

My step-mom rubbed my shoulder compassionately as we walked home; she'd seen it all.

My dad said "See, he did great while we were in there. Just tell him what he has to do and he will listen."

I was so mad. I thought to myself, *I am a terrible mom if this is what I am supposed to do naturally but it seems to exhaust me. What if, one day, I didn't do any of these preventative measures and everyone saw what he was really like? Would they then know what I had to do all the time and validate it?* I knew in my heart that my sacrifice for everyone seeing that would be embarrassing for my family and, most of all, my son. I cried after the ceremony; my stepmom saw it all and said how amazing I was doing. She approached me when we got home, grabbed my shoulders and looked me in the eyes with a sincere look and said "Oh, you poor girl. I see how much you do with him and you work so hard. I want you to know that I see he is doing well because of the amount of work you do with him. I am proud of you. I just wanted you to know that." I instantly burst into tears and cried while she held me while I let go of the exhaustion into her deep loving hug. I felt her love and support, and in that moment, she gave me the strength to keep moving on.

CHAPTER 6

PERSPECTIVES

MAYBE SCOTT WAS just like I was when I was younger? After all, my nickname as a child was Tararizer. Maybe my son was just like me and this is normal. My mom never said I was difficult. No one ever said anything about my active boy. Our families never mentioned that Scott had "too much" energy. My uncle called him "Gotta Go" when he met him, but that was it. My mom loves being a grandma. When we visited the farm, she would give Scott anything he wanted and let him run free. Nana loves her little Scotty so much she could never say anything was wrong with him. She would always just applaud how great he was. Scott was her first grandchild from her second born daughter so she was absolutely smitten with him. Whenever I would suggest I was struggling, she would slough it off because to her Scott was perfect the way he was.

Jack and I had decided to not live close to our families because we didn't want their opinions to affect our relationship. I come from a big family. I have seven step-siblings, one half sister and one full sister. Jack on the other hand only has one full blood sister. Ultimately, living further way from my family was a way to prevent any drama and exposure into our lives because we could monitor how often we wanted to talk to anyone. I made sure I never shared anything with my family about my life because I always wanted them to think I was doing well, so I wasn't the topic of gossip or conversation in my family. The less they worried about me the better because I was always a rock in our family. I didn't want to seem like I wasn't as strong as everyone thought I was. Jack and I had a fairy-tale relationship, in the beginning, a superficial fantasy. We liked to drink beer, eat chicken wings and planned spontaneous fun things to do. A stress free fairy-tale without minimal close friends or family. It sounded perfect to us at the time. When we started to have trouble with Scott, I refused to appear weak in the eyes of my family. I didn't need seven different opinions on how to parent. If one of my siblings knew; they all knew. No one can keep a secret in my family because they all want to be helpful or right.

My parents divorced when I was younger and when we visited my dad, he would say I needed to be stricter with Scott and that he needed spankings. My dad was able to see the defiance in Scott, but he thought it was because he was from a different generation, and that my generation does not support spankings. I have heard that from lots of people; they assume that people who work in human services do not support spankings, but what most people don't know is that new law came out a while ago that stated spankings are ok when they are safe and done over a layer of clothing with an open hand. I grew up with safe spankings and I saw nothing wrong with using them on my children. However when I shared with my Dad that Scott punched me after I spanked him he looked shocked, but he still reiterated that I needed to be more strict with him. It felt like he never heard what I told him. *What would being more strict look like, I was already very strict. I never backed down on a consequence and I always made sure there were lessons learned.*

Jack's mother assured me Scott was fine. When I suggested she take the leash with her when she watched him, she refused it. Then, we'd get a panicked call from her when she lost him in the grocery store. This was her first grandchild and she was coming from a loving perspective. It had been a long time since she'd been a new mother herself, so she didn't know if Scott's behaviour was "normal" or not. Eventually, she told us she was getting too old to be able to watch him as much.

Jack's sister and her husband just listened to me talk about my problems without judgment. They never suggested anything either way when I would talk about Scott's energy. They were the only two that did not hold a judgement look on their faces when I would share with people the little things, hoping someone would step in and say something.

I felt so much shame about my "problem" that I pretty much isolated myself and didn't share with my family about what was going on for me. It's no wonder I didn't know what they were thinking, or even if they were thinking anything about what kind of behaviours Scott was exhibiting.

I had just started a few good friendships with some females in my life at this point, but I isolated myself from them too. I always cancelled my plans with them and made excuses on why I was not able to hang out.

My coworkers had no clue because I didn't talk about anything I struggled with in any area of my life, so they didn't see or notice anything new in me. They were all very warm and welcoming of Scott and I into their lives, but I never brought up what was truly going on for me.

Jack was adamant that Scott's behaviours were no big deal and that he would grow out of them, why should I try to convince my family that I believed there was something wrong. I was never one to ask for help, but welcomed it when someone offered. I felt bad for leaving my family out. I had a huge family and I know my siblings and everyone else also needed my parents' support. How could I expect them to help when they lived as far away as they did? Maybe I would have reached out for help if I hadn't been trying to be so strong. When my sisters would call and talk about their day, I listened and offered support rather than sharing my own sob story. No one knew the truth because I didn't share it. I never wanted to look like a terrible mother because I felt like one.

Our friends were having more children at this point and for me there was no way I felt that I should ever be having another child. Look what I had done to this child. My focus was to fix what I'd done. My husband asked me if I wanted more children. I said, "No. Never again! I am not meant to be a mom." I needed to fix what I had done first. Jack and I went as far as getting a vasectomy.

I felt like a failure as a mom and a failure as a wife. I felt so bad that my husband had picked me to have a child and a life with. At work, I see kids all of the time with attachment issues. You know, the ones that aren't shy with other adults and run into their arms. These kids that run into the arms of people they just met means that they have not had their mother or father show love and care for them enough in their short lives for them to feel secure in love. My son was acting just like those children that I'd seen at work that had been taken from their parents' care or who had parents that didn't love them and treat them right. His behaviours were exactly as if he had an attachment reactive disorder, as if his process of attachment to me had been disrupted. He was showing signs that I never loved him enough. From my education and experience I have learned that at the developmental age of eighteen months, children should be scared of strangers, but that's positive because they are building strong attachments to their parents. Scott at that age would run away from me and sit on a complete stranger's lap. One time I found him on a big burly scary looking man's lap in the middle of a mall. Most people find it sweet and cute because most people don't realize it's a red flag that they are not attached to their current caregiver, and in Scott's case.... That was me. *How could this be possible? What have I done?* No one knew how much of a failure I felt like. I suffered in silence.

CHAPTER 7

INCIDENTS

SCOTT WAS THREE years old when I started having to sign daily incident reports regarding his behaviour. The themes, over and over: "Scott intentionally does not listen to the staff; he runs away and laughs while he does it; he hugs kids when they don't want to be hugged" and on and on. The reports flowed through my hands so often I just signed and went on with the evening.

One day, Scott reportedly touched a girl inappropriately. Since my son was only three, I asked for more clarity. The incident report from the daycare said he went into the bathroom and helped a little girl pull up her underwear and pants. I was confused, but the staff was adamant that it was completely inappropriate.

Jack and I asked for a meeting with the director of the daycare.

"I am happy you called this meeting, we also have some concerns we have wanted to talk to you guys about" Said the Director starting our meeting.

"We have completed his Ages and Stages Questionnaire that shows if he is developmentally on par for his age. Most areas he did well, but we are concerned about the social and emotional development of your son."

Jacks body immediately tensed up "Oh really" he said. "And what exactly does that mean or look like?"

"Well" she proceeded "He is lacking in his compassion, he has no remorse when he injures another child. He has no respect for other people's space, even when they tell him to stop he doesn't. He hugs children all of the time, but to the point where he annoys the other children and he will end up hurting them with his hugs. He runs away from us all of the time to the point where we basically need a one to one staff for him and when we tell him 'no' he does it anyway. He knows exactly what he is doing."

My heart melted when I heard her talk. I knew what she was talking about because I experienced the same things. Jack only focused on his son not being labelled as a sexual predator and sternly responded "But, we can both agree that he was not touching that little girl in a sexual nature and that you could re-word that incident report your staff wrote."

"Yes", she said "but I want you to think about what I have just shared and how concerned we are about your son."

"Sure." Jack replied.

The second we got out of the meeting Jack started ranting about how terrible of a daycare that was and that we needed to start looking for a different daycare to watch our son. I didn't share with Jack at that time how I felt because he was so upset. But deep down inside, I felt the same way they did. It hurt me to hear that they ultimately didn't like my son.

Jack had trouble accepting that there was anything wrong with his son; he was Scott's biggest advocate, believing he was perfectly normal. I agreed that he hadn't intended to violate a little girl, so wasn't convinced the daycare was a reliable source of recognizing any wrong-doing. I still felt like I was the reason he was doing what he was doing. If my husband couldn't see it… then it had to be me. I was the only one present for all of the meltdowns. I was still struggling to make sense of it. Secretly in my head, I was apologizing to my husband for being the reason for this, and I was sorry for raising our son into a boy who was struggling in his relationships with his peers.

Scott had stitches twice already from running and falling. I had never had stitches in my life, but my husband reassured me that it was normal for boys to have stitches. My husband got them lots while playing hockey, but Scott wasn't in hockey yet.

When Scott had to get stitches on his forehead, I met the director of the daycare at the hospital. She looked exhausted. I wondered if that was what I looked like. I'll never forget the look she gave me when she said, "Your son climbed up the monkey bars after I told him not too. He deliberately disobeyed me. We can't keep chasing him all over the place while looking after the other children."

The daycare didn't like him. So, I agreed with Jack it was finally time to find a different daycare or send him to preschool while I finished the attachment work. I was hell bent on learning to be a better mom. Meanwhile, my son was running around the hospital with blood dripping from his open wound. I apologized to the director and she left while I stayed with Scott. When the nurse saw how active Scott was she said that they would have to be rough to get his eighteen stitches in. She said, "You might want to leave for this, we will need to use a bedsheet to wrap him up in it like a straight jacket."

"Ok, I'll get him" I grabbed him and held his arms around him while I sat with him trying to hold his legs. "Scott, we need to get your sore closed so it can heal, If you can't sit still we will need to continue to hold you." I said

"Nooooo let go of me mom"

"No, Scott, we need to do this." Instantly there were three nurses there who started to roll him up in the sheet just like a mummy.

"Stop it" he would scream while his face got red and started banging it back and forth.

Successfully, he was starting to unravel the cloth, so I grabbed his legs and the nurses called for other nurses to help. Two more nurses came to the room and I held him tight while they all put the sheet back on him in a full body hold. He started to bite my arms. One nurse said hurry up people the mom is starting to draw blood from the bite. They all quickly worked together and I was able to let go while the nurses stood around the bed, so he didn't fall off. The doctor came in and said "ok we have to work quickly on this child. One nurse said they wouldn't have been able to get him in the sheet if it wasn't for the mom holding him. The doctor looked at me with a raised eyebrow and said "Oh, we normally don't have kids with this amount of energy have their moms help because its too hard to watch their kids get wrapped up. Normally we don't put them in sheets like we have had to do with your son, but thank you I can't imagine how this was something you were able to do. I will work quickly."

As I waited for them to finish I started thinking … *Maybe I had been too cold. How could a mother help hold her son down without shedding one single tear?*

At work, I had discovered this expert who works with children and youth who are severely impacted with attachment and trauma issues her name is Tracy Cook. I got to see the work that she did when I visited her group homes. This is where I learned a little bit about time-ins. I was no expert, but I learned that when children have trauma and attachment issues, time-ins are used; this form of discipline reinforces that the caregiver/

parent/support staff will always be there for the child and there is no fear of losing love or struggling alone. Severely traumatized children need to be reassured. I thought Scott would benefit from the same because his behaviours were the same. I opened up to Tracy one day while over the phone.

"Tracy, can I ask a personal question, its about my son"

"Sure, Tara we have worked together for a long time if I can help with anything I am here"

"Well the thing is, I am starting to get daily phone calls from the daycare about things they are worried about. They say he is different than the other children and they are worried about how he is acting." I vaguely said.

"Hahahaha, Tara, he is going to be ok with you as a mom. Just start working on giving him positive reinforcement on the things he does well right now to build up his character that way, your son hasn't been severely traumatized and has a mom who truly loves and cares for him, so have faith in yourself. He is young Tara, so I wouldn't be too worried about it just yet."

Regardless of hearing her say I would be ok, I didn't have faith in myself. I didn't feel hopeful. I needed more support, but I never told her that. I felt that there was more going on for him, so I decided to take Gordon Neufelds Intentensive Course Level One for aggressive children to explain to me how to manage attachment issues in children. I needed to understand where Scott's anger, anxiety and disregard for adult direction originated so I could bridge his attachment to me. I was convinced I was the reason because I had to be rough with him after his birth in order to get him to eat. That must have caused me to disengage from him and I needed to understand how to bring him back. I could fix this… I needed to fix this.

CHAPTER 8

UNPREDICTABLE

JACK WORKED AWAY in a city that was two hours away from us, so it was just Scott and me most of the time. Jack had made a career change and we had invested in a business that he spent long hours working at. It consumed most of his time. I had friends whose husbands also worked away and I always heard it was more difficult when the fathers came home because it disrupted the routine. Scott and I had a simple routine in place. This minimized the chances of a meltdown. I kept everything as predictable for him as I could. Scott did better when we did the same thing everyday. Scott loved to ride on his car, and watch The Lion King over and over again.

Jack came home on the weekends and it disrupted our carefully designed routine. One Friday night, I walked in to Scott's bedroom to see them wrestling with each other. Scott's laugh got higher and higher. I felt the urge to tell them to stop, but they were having so much fun. Scott started to climb all over his dad. Then Jack abruptly told him that was enough and it was time for bed. Scott said "NO" and kept trying to jump on Jacks back. Jack pulled him off of his back and Jack started to walk away. I caught a glimpse of the look of vengeance that Scott got in his eye then he disappeared into his closet. This was a vengeful look that I was familiar with, but Jack was not. Jack was already in the kitchen when Scott came running after him with a metal hanger and he hit Jack as hard as he could with the hanger against his back. Jack yelped out in pain. Scott just gave a smirk of satisfaction on his face. Jack said "THAT'S IT! Time out in your room Scott." He picked up Scott and carried him over his shoulders. Scott continued to close fist punch Jack on the back over and over again while he carried him to Scott's room. He put Scott on the bed and held the door closed. The banging and crashing from his room continued for a few hours. He would scream "I hate you dad" "you're going to get it dad" while he held the door closed. I was so furious. I knew it could have been prevented, but Jack didn't see that he did anything wrong because it was Scott who shouldn't behave like that. I felt terrible that all I wanted was for Jack to go back to work.

How much wrestling and fun could he take before it got out of control? I had no real solution to disciplining him when "fun" got to be too much for him. I didn't want positive experiences to be remembered for their negative outcomes. So, I knew that I needed to be in more control and limit the fun that Scott was able to have since he could never be excited and calm himself back down.

I started to understand Scott's triggers and how avoid them. I would need to tell him exactly what we were doing at all times. I never allowed him to play too much, and I was very strict with our schedule. The only thing that calmed him down was watching TV. Which confused me because stimulating him would be overwhelming, how was TV able to keep him still, but things were quiet during those moments and I could relax and let go of trying to control every single second of every single day for

Scott. I knew too much screen time wasn't good for children, but it was the only thing that I could use as a bargaining chip. It gave me a sense of calm to have control over something that mattered to him. I knew I needed a better strategy for consequences because his hitting would become unmanageable as he got older, bigger and stronger.

Now that I was working on our relationship, I could incorporate time-ins as a regular discipline strategy. A "time-in" is when a parent or caregiver removes the child from a situation in which he is melting down and stays with them. While you hold the childs arms around themselves, similar to a straight jacket while repeating out loud: "You are not in control of yourself right now." I never witnessed Scott to have any strong emotions until I started using this strategy. This hold made Scott so mad that he would scratch and bite me in the hopes of being released. I would hold it until he wore out, his body would slowly get exhausted fighting so hard to get out of the hold that eventually he would give in and we could move on. He would never apologize for hurting me or break into tears of sadness, but it would stop him from being aggressive.

He couldn't stand losing control. It got worse. He would scream in terror as I was holding him.

"I am going to kill you when you let go of me"

"I hope I make you bleed"

"You will pay for this"

"I just want to rip your face off"

It was hard to hear my son scream such terrible words, but I thought the hold was better than him violently hitting me with his fists and with hangers. He started to test me daily if I gave him a time-in. At one point when he was mad that day or didn't get his own way, he would grab breakable items I cared about or his own stuff and break it right in front of me to see what I would do. I had to remain consistent, so I showed him that was how I would give him consequences. He was no longer hurting me, but he was in the testing phase. The hardest part of his testing phase was the second we were done the hold he would blame me and yell at me for making him break his toys and the stuff he cares about.

One day, I put him into the hold like I had so many times previously but, this time, my soul couldn't handle it. He was trying to bite my face as he scratched my arms until they bled. While he was physically terrorizing me, he threatened me in a deep angry voice: "I'm going to kill you and tear off your skin." I could see in his eyes that he wanted to cause me pain while he was gouging my skin out. It was like he was possessed.

I couldn't see any light at the end of the tunnel. If I let him go before he was finished melting down, he would destroy the house, break his own toys, or keep punching me. I did let him go before he was fully exhausted one time and he went straight to the bathroom and ripped the towel rack off the wall. He was wildly unpredictable.

How can this ever result in anything good? What else am I supposed to do? Am I actually supporting him through his meltdowns or am I creating what will be a bigger monster later?.

Every single time he was done with his meltdowns, he would be devastated that he had broken his toys, and damaged things in the house. He blamed me for making him wreck his things. According to him, it was always my fault for making him mad.

These outbursts happened about three times a week and went on for a full year. It was hard to not taken them personally when they were directed at me. However, I was consistent with my discipline and after a while, Scott started to listen better.

We started Scott in hockey during this time because

keeping him active seemed like the best thing to do. Jack was now able to coach Scott's team since we made the decision to move a bit closer to Jack's work so that he could be home at nights. His daily commute was one hour one way now and even though he wouldn't be home for supper, he could be home to tuck Scott in. He was also able to leave work early on the days of practice to meet me at the rink for practice and games. From the moment I picked Scott up from daycare, he would scream and tell me he didn't want to go to hockey. No one else was there to see the fight to get him to the rink. Everyone would just say it was normal for kids to not want to engage in team sports at first, but you just have to keep making them go. I did. But Scott kept hitting and yelling at me all the way to practice. Then I had to deal with the meltdown after.

When I got him to the rink, he wouldn't listen to the coaches but would do whatever he wanted to do. He would get mad over a variety of things: he couldn't skate fast enough; his friends didn't pass him the puck; he didn't like the practices; he only wanted to play games, etc. He was a poor sport. Every day after practice, he would have a meltdown or have to leave practice early because he was getting sweaty under his helmet and he didn't like that feeling. It was a terrible experience for us both, but his dad really wanted him to be the type of son who loved to play competitive hockey. I hated being the one who had to deal with Scott's clear distaste for getting sweaty and hot.

I stuck it out for two very long years from age three to age five, finally, I was done.

Jack's heart broke when I told him I couldn't take Scott to hockey anymore. He was proud to be a hockey dad—even if Scott clearly didn't like playing a team sport. We needed to find a different sport for Scott and Jack needed to accept that his son wouldn't be a hockey player. If I learned anything about a father's love during this time, it was that it's more difficult for a man to accept his son as being different than it is for a mother. My heart broke for Scott and his father. Jack's love for his son had him convinced that the situation would get better. For Jack, staying in denial and hoping Scott would grow out of all of his behaviours made it easier on Jack.

One day when we were visiting Jack's sister and mom, I decided to be completely honest with them about how Scott was doing at hockey.

"Well, Scott doesn't actually like going to hockey. He does his own thing on the ice during practice. When the coaches tell him what to do, he just skates away and does what he wants. The last practice, he had to leave the ice because he was refusing to practice. I met him in the dressing room and he started screaming and thrashing his body against the walls. When I finally got his helmet off he said it was because he was sweating and he hates being sweaty." I shared "But, it was a hard day and I don't understand why he can't do practice like the other kids."

"Scott has always been different than the other kids though" Jacks sister shared.

"Really" I said… "You see how he is different?"

"Yes, we love him and he is perfect, but he doesn't play the same as other kids, but you knew that already right?"

I burst out into tears at the table and responded in between sobbing, "Thank you for sharing that, I thought I was the only one who saw that he was different. Jack doesn't see it either, so I thought it was just me."

She gave me the biggest hug and held me while I cried.

"Oh Tara, yes my husband and I have seen it and we are here if you need us."

I felt such a huge sense of relief in knowing she had seen that Scott was different than the other children since she had children of her own as well. This meant that it wasn't me who needed work on my parenting. Now I could shift gears from thinking I was the problem. I was terrified to parent more children in the event it was my parenting that caused all of what Scotty was going through. It was in that moment I realized I could mother another child.

CHAPTER 9

A NEW BEGINNING

JACK HAD GOTTEN a vasectomy a year after Scott was born but, after we discussed it, Jack agreed to go for a reversal so we could try for another child. Merely two months after the reversal, we were pregnant again! We were shocked at how fast that was since Jack and I were told potentially we would not be able to conceive again knowing we did a vasectomy. When we told Scott he would be a big brother, he was excited. He told us that he wanted a sister. When we tried to explain that we didn't know the gender of the baby yet, Scott was still sure I had a girl in my tummy. Jack and I decided that to help Scott with the process we would find out the gender in the event it was a boy he would have time to accept and process it. We had someone make cake pops with the colour pink or blue and we would bite into them to find out the gender of our baby. We were excited to do it with Scott.

"Ok Scott, so when you bite into this cake pop if its pink you will have a little sister and if its blue you will have a brother." I explained.

Looking at them he said "Give me the pink one because I know it's a girl."

"That's not how it works hunny, but just bite into this and we can talk about it." I gave him the first cake pop.

He took a bite and it was pink on the inside, "See mom, I told you it was going to be a sister." He was so sure the entire time. Which was good because he accepted being a big brother a lot better than we had anticipated. I was excited for the pregnancy until a wave of anxiety flooded over me out of fear that the second child might be exactly like Scott. Scott was now four years old, and I knew what to expect for him, but I wasn't sure what the next child would be like. I was six months pregnant and it had been a long day at work. All I wanted to do was go home and put my feet up, but we needed groceries. I picked Scott up and headed to the grocery store.

While we were there, Scott ran away twice. So, I just left the cart with the groceries in it and carried him out screaming. I put him in the truck but he was so hysterical that I couldn't do up his seat belt; so I left him alone for a bit. He was screaming so loud that people were staring at me. I opened the door to do up his seatbelt, and he screamed that he would kill me and started kicking and punching me. I closed the door. How was I going to drive home without him buckled?

I went back in and tried to force him into his seat. He bit me so hard I started to cry, so I immediately closed the door and left. He started smashing the windows with his seatbelt buckle. All I could do was cry. I called Jack even though he was working out of town. He listened to me cry because that's all he could do. Every time I opened the door, Scott would smack me on the face or kick my pregnant stomach. After twenty minutes of Scott continuing to do this over and over again without settling down, I decided to get back in behind the wheel and, against all maternal instinct I said, "STOP IT OR I'M LEAVING YOU HERE ALL BY YOURSELF."

He instantly started crying and wouldn't stop. He cried so much that his little body went soft and I could finally buckle him up. He cried for the entire forty-five minute drive home. "You were going to leave me," he sputtered. "You don't love me. More snivelling. "I would have died, Mom. Does that make you happy?"

I felt myself slowly die inside that my son thought that was how I felt about him. As I sat in the face of his accusations, I felt shame and fear about raising another child. I let my son beat me up because I could take it, but there was no way I could let him do that to my unborn child, or later to his baby sibling. I was terrified. How was I going to protect the newborn from Scott?

CHAPTER 10

DEFINING MOMENT

JACK AND I decided to put him into preschool at age four to see how he did in social situations with peers since the daycare was an epic failure and he would soon be a big brother. I told the preschool teacher on the first day that he was struggling with some behaviours and I had talked to an attachment specialist. I told her I was working on some parenting strategies I had learned in an attachment course. I told her that when I found out more, or if she saw things she wanted to share, we should be in touch. We would be in constant communication for Scott's success. It was a wonderful meeting.

I was thrown completely off when, three months into preschool, I got a shocking call that I will never forget. There was nothing different about the day until my phone rang.

"Hi, my name is Samantha and I am a social worker; I am on my way to your home to interview your child, Scott, about a report we received. Are you able to meet me there in about an hour? I know it's hard to believe right now, but I will be expecting to meet you there." She said with a soft and gentle voice.

I paused…. In disbelief. "Is this a joke?"

"I'm afraid not Tara." She replied

"Ok, I guess I'll grab Scott and meet you there?" I hung up the phone and just stood there trying to process if it was joke or not. However, the phone never rang again, so I grabbed my coat and told my supervisor that a social worker was on their way to interview Scott and I didn't understand. She looked very confused as well. My supervisor was a huge support to me and was someone who I deeply respected. She personally knew my son and I both.

I left to pick up Scott. When I got to the preschool, the preschool teacher pulled me aside and she looked worried.

"I am so sorry Tara; it's my fault why someone is coming to your place. I didn't mean for this to happen. I called a social worker because another child was saying he gets hit on the head and Scott repeated him. I know you said you were getting support, and I didn't know if I should call or not. I have a friend, who works there, and I wanted to talk to her, but they put me through to someone else and it all happened so fast. The person coming to your house just called me; I told her that she should NOT be going to your home, but I couldn't stop her. I am so so sorry". She said while tears were rolling down her face.

I didn't know what to say. I was in shock. I mustered up a response "that's ok." I said. Tears started to form in my eyes. I grabbed Scott and headed home. I didn't say anything to Scott.

When the assessor knocked on the door, I asked her why she was coming out to my place and what the concern was. She said she needed to interview Scott before informing me of the complaint. I know that Children Services Social Workers have the right to come into your home, interview your children alone; they have the authority to do it. It was hard letting her into my home to do that, but I knew I had no rights or choice at this point. I took her and Scott upstairs and gave him his snack and told him that she wanted to talk to him. I left the area and sat at the table; I waited patiently. It felt like forever,

Defining Moment

but she eventually came down the stairs and sat at the table with me.

"Scott has a lot of energy." She said.

"Yes he does I said. Now can you help me understand why you had to interview him?" I asked

"Well, she said we got a report that Scott said he gets hit on the head."

All I could think was, there was no way of her knowing that I do not hit our son, but how could I prove that to her that it wasn't true?"

I asked, "How could someone who has no criminal records and no history of children services result in someone coming to interview their child. I know that people can call in on people all of the time, but that there is a period to assess if you need to go to their homes or if you need to talk to the kids or not. Is there more information that I don't know about?"

She responded" We didn't call anyone to verify if you were an appropriate parent or not because we didn't want to impact you more by calling the school etc because then they would be aware that we were called."

" Thanks for being kind." I said, "But, I know who called. It was our preschool teacher, so the reality is you already knew the school knew. The preschool teacher told me that you were on your way. She told me she just called a social worker to ask if she should make a report because Scott repeated the sentence that he gets hit on the head after another child in his class said it. She said he was laughing and joking when he said it, but she wasn't concerned enough for someone to come and look into me. She also told me that she was hoping to talk to a friend she knew, but instead she got sent to a place where she had to share it like a report. Now tell me" I said to her " How could it still result in you coming to our place when the person who called in herself apologized to me and told me she told you she didn't think it actually happened?" I was upset and starting to get angry.

"It was a report of abuse, so we had to look into it." She said.

"And, what is your conclusion?" I asked.

"My conclusion is that the concerns are unsubstantiated. So, that means it was a false report. Scott didn't share any concerns about how discipline is handled or even any worries he has. Scott has a lot of energy and is hard to understand as well. I am sorry to have bothered you Tara, but thank you for your time." She stated. And just like that, she was gone. As I watched her drive away, I burst out into tears. I was so embarrassed and ashamed that she had been at my house in a professional manner.

How could I go back to work in Human Services being on the other side of the coin? The shame was so large I cried.....I cried for months. I took a medical leave from work. I was too ashamed to look my supervisor in the eyes or to be in families homes and interview their children now that I had felt what it feels like because they had to see if I was keeping my child safe. I decided that I would fight hard. I formally requested all of the details from our file to find out what and why it had happened. Maybe there were lots of more reports that people made that I was not aware of. I needed to see my file and the information the government had on me and my son who now had an official identification in the children services system. He wouldn't have existed in the system before this, but now he did. I thought maybe if I could have it removed it would make me feel better.

Once I got the file information that I requested from the government I shared the detailed file information with my most recent supervisor. I shared it for her advice, but I also shared it so she could see that I have never hurt little Scotty. Since she knew a social worker was at my house, I wanted her to see the truth on what the investigator wrote on the computer system. I also wanted to share it so I did not lose my job or career from it. She said that considering how difficult Scott is it's better to leave the information on the government computer system rather than a clean slate. Her rationale was that if Scott has made one allegation, it's more likely he will make another one in the future. They will have a record of all of the work I was doing as a parent of a difficult child. It made me sick knowing that leaving it alone and NOT fighting against the government body to have it removed was likely the best thing for us. I didn't even know why Scott would have said what he did. It was then that I realized we needed to seek out professional support for Scott, knowing that I was a "normal" good parent. I knew someone through work who would do a neuropsychological assessment of him and Jack and I paid for it out of pocket after the birth of our second child. She was due to come in less than two months from now. I decided to include this episode in the book because maybe, just maybe, there are others who are, or will be, in the same, or similar, situation and need to hear this message: You're not alone.

Jack was now ready to accept that maybe there was something that was different about Scott because he knows I have never hit Scott and so why would Scott even say something like that or repeat the statement after another child.

CHAPTER 11

FINALLY

WHEN MY SECOND child was born, Layla, and she made eye contact with me. I cried. She was "normal." After all the years of frustration, and more recently the troublesome weeks of tears, I felt relief. It wasn't me that wasn't able to connect with Scott. I had no measuring stick for Scott when he was born because he was my first child. If I had given birth to Layla before Scott, I would have instantly known when Scott was born that something was different because he looked through me and not at me. I would have never had to go through the journey of thinking there was something wrong with me as a parent for as long as I did because I did not know what was normal for babies. Layla was beautiful, perfect and I made sure to keep her with me at all times, that way, I never had to worry about Scott because she was on me like an accessory. Scotty liked Layla and loved making her smile, but I was still cautious. Shockingly, he was an amazing big brother. I chose to have a c-section with Layla because I was terrified of repeating the same labour story as Scott's. For the first five weeks after a c-section you're supposed to not lift too much or do too much because it could ruin your healing time. C-sections are surgeries so the recovery time is the same. After only being home for three days, I had just finished breast feeding Layla when I saw Scott running down the road out the window. That was the first time I had to leave Layla alone in the house by herself while I ran after Scott to save his life. I cried while I was running and holding my incision. I was starting to bleed and hurt, but I had to catch Scott before he got severely hurt. The second we got back home, I realized it was finally time to get Scott a neuropsychological assessment. At work there were a few psychologists who were doctors that we used for assessments, so I knew exactly who I wanted to use. I had read this doctors work many times, so I knew his work. I knew we could have gone through our doctor and wait for the recommendation to get an assessment, but those free services for families have waitlists up to two years. I was not willing to wait for help.

Scott had just turned five years old and to avoid any future mishaps, we paid three thousand dollars for this service. It was more than worth it. Scott was diagnosed with Attention Deficit Hyperactivity Disorder (ADHD).

Through the assessment phase, the doctor, compiled information from the school and the kindergarten teacher who stated the same worries I had: Scott had punched the teacher and ran away when he was frustrated, he did not stop when he was asked to stop, he was constantly asking what they were doing next and he always had to know, etc. A wave of understanding and emotion took over me. It was not just me and now everyone was starting to see it in many different environments. My son was actually struggling with something inside himself. I had no idea the school teachers were seeing the same things I was. They never called or shared that information with Jack or I. I wept for days with relief. I had answers. The doctor said that we needed to start the ADHD medication and that once it was under control, they may discover some underlying issues. Finally, there were steps to take. We had to see a psychiatrist to get medication.

While we waited months for our appointment, I tracked all of Scott's behaviours right from the DSM-IV. The Diagnostic and Statistical Manual of Mental Disorders is a publication used by doctors to classify and diagnose mental disorders using common language and standard criteria in an attempt to give as much information to our psychiatrist as I could. I made sure to track each and every symptom of ADHD and Oppositional Defiance Disorder (ODD). I knew from my experience at work that sometimes children were diagnosed with both of them and, since he didn't listen to any authority figures, I made sure to document it all.

CHAPTER 12

TRIAL AND ERROR

THE DAY OF our appointment finally arrived and I was ready. I had pages and pages of documentation for every type of behaviour I had seen from Scott in the past couple of months. As prepared as I was for the conversation, I never expected it to be one of the worst appointments I had ever attended. The psychiatrist asked us very personal questions about Scott's behaviours that were difficult to answer with Scott present. He said he needed the child present for the appointments. Scott struggled to stay in the room and wanted to leave when we started to talk about him. I held Scott's head between my hands and said, "Look at my eyes." I waited for him to make eye contact. He looked at me and I said, "Mommy and Daddy are going to talk to this doctor about some of the things you do, but remember we love you and we love your brain."

He said, "Okay," and calmed down a bit, but still ran around the room.

We weren't in the office for more than ten minutes and Scott was diagnosed with Oppositional Defiance Disorder as well. The psychiatrist didn't even look at my notes. It had taken thousands of dollars and tons of information to diagnose him with ADHD, but only ten minutes for an ODD diagnosis. I was surprised at how fast he was able to do that. Jack stayed quiet while I shared all of my documentation. The psychiatrist gave us our first ADHD prescription called Concerta.

After the appointment Jack struggled with the additional diagnosis, but told me he trusted me to track and follow-up with what was best for Scott. So, we started with ADHD medication. Finally, we had meds. I was sure they would fix everything.

First, we started with Concerta. It was a long-lasting medication that would stay in his system all day. It worked instantly: he could focus and sit still, but he couldn't sleep. No one told us that he would stay awake for two full weeks with insomnia. I started to read … and read … and read. I was consumed with understanding what was going on. I needed to share it with the doctor. We increased the medication three times, for three weeks at a time, until we changed to a different medication: Vyvanse. No more insomnia. But he was so goofy that he couldn't control himself. It was weird because he acted like a different child, but he was no longer running as much. Or so I thought, until we took him to a hockey game at the Calgary Saddledome. Scott sat like a well-behaved child until the third period. I had Layla in a carrier on my chest and I took Scott into the foyer to stretch his legs. I told him, "We can play a game. I will say 'GO' and you run until I say 'STOP' after three seconds." He agreed.

We played it over and over and over again. He listened and followed my directions every single time; but I didn't expect the buzzer to go the second after I said "GO." Scott was gone like a flash into the crowd of people exiting the seating area. He would not have heard me count and he never came back. I

Trial and Error

ran frantically through the crowd of people leaving the stadium. I started aggressively pushing them out of the way yelling for Scott. I ran all the way through the entire stadium and there was no Scott in sight. The panic stopped and fear took over. I had no idea where to look. Tears of terror started pouring out of me as I ran around the stadium.

I finally spotted him with my sister-in-law and Jack in the exact spot we had started from. Scott looked at me and said, "I won!" I grabbed him and held him tight with relief. He had no fear, no idea about the impact his running by himself through a stadium of people could be. It's was like he had no idea he'd done anything wrong. Jack was devastated that I lost Scott in the crowd of people, but since he only knew about it when he was found he wasn't as upset as I was. Jack didn't blame me for it since he knew Scott was hard to keep still. We both agreed we would share the incident with the doctor on the next appt.

When we shared our recent incident with the doctor, he said, "Well, maybe the medication dose wasn't high enough."

It's amazing how long you can go between doctor's visits and increases in medication before trying a different kind.

Because I was tracking daily symptoms and behaviours for a few months, I became an expert on Scott and the different types of ADHD medication, to the point where the doctor was insulted when I asked for a different medication or to increase the dosage of the current one. Finally, I told him Concerta was better if we had a higher dose … maybe. I didn't want to try the shorter-acting medication because I would have to go to the school to give it to Scott during the day. I didn't want people thinking he was any different or the school to judge me because my five-year-old was on medication. Back to Concerta.

Scott focused like crazy. Days were good and his nights were better because we started to use Melatonin to help him sleep. But Melatonin was only to be used on a short-term basis and was not a long-term solution. Soon, the only problem was that he was hyper-focused sometimes. He would be difficult to change activities most days, but now when he was organizing cars or sorting anything he couldn't do what you asked until it was completely done. If we forced him to change tasks he would scream and punch. Even though I struggled with managing his hyper-focusing, I thought for sure that it was better for him at school now because he would be getting his school work done, but his meltdowns only continued at home ... they slowly got worse.

CHAPTER 13

MARRIAGE

THE DAY STARTED like any other day. I picked up Scott from school he was grumpy and didn't want to buckle his seatbelt up like usual. I had to lean my weight onto him every day in order to buckle him up. When I asked him about his day, he would usually yell, "IT WAS FINE." That was our normal. When we got home, I quickly went about making supper. I loathed supper time and even more so on the days that Jack made it home in time for supper. Scott would never simply sit down and eat. He was always getting up and moving around. He was a fussy eater. He didn't like any sauces and his food couldn't touch. I had to make his food as plain as possible, then maybe add something extra and interesting for my husband and me. Jack couldn't stand it that his son wouldn't just sit and eat. I got used to it, so I didn't make it the hill I died on because it would result in another meltdown and a rough night.

Jack got so mad that Scott wasn't eating supper one time, that he told him to go to his room for a time-out. Scott went to his room, but came right back out. So, I did the time-in, holding him in his room. He started to scratch me. Jack had never witnessed what Scott does when I would hold him; he intervened this time because he didn't like to see me get hurt especially from our own child. I always hid the scratches I had in the past from him because I didn't want him to worry. So, this time, he grabbed Scott and yelled, "YOU NEED A TIME OUT."

We lived on an acreage, so he put him outside on the deck for a breather, which was safe because there were no roads nearby. We locked eyes as he closed the front door on Scotty. I felt like he understood: We were lost and frustrated parents with a six-year-old child running our house. We were trying everything.

Back in "the old days" they would have taken him out of school, beat him, and put him to work on the farm. Then he would turn into that teenager who killed his family. Then, AND ONLY THEN, would the community say, "Oh yeah, we knew there was something off about that kid." That terrified me.

Jack and I sat in silence with our own thoughts while Scott was outside screaming that he was going to kill us. We heard a loud smash coming from our living room. Scott had taken one of Jack's steel toe boots and thrown it at the window. It shattered. We leapt up and went outside to grab him so he wouldn't hurt himself with the glass. The glass breaking shocked Scott so much he stopped screaming.

Jack carried Scott to the kitchen table and made him sit down. He sternly instructed Scott to eat. Scott ate, but with a glare on his face. We put him straight to bed after supper.

As I lay in bed, I fretted about how I was going to handle supper the next night. Because tomorrow, he wouldn't be able to sit at the table for supper again. He never does. It was a battle I was going to have to fight every night now. I stopped caring about him sitting still at the dinner table, but now since Jack had put his foot down that Scott needed to sit while eating my hands were tied on enforcing that rule whether Jack was home for supper or not. I was terrified that our three-times-a-week meltdowns were now going to increase to every night regardless of him being on ADHD medication. Feeling helpless, I silently cried myself to sleep.

CHAPTER 14

FRUSTRATION

AT OUR NEXT psychiatrist's appt, we shared our worries about Scott's meltdowns and his inability to turn his defiance around. The psychiatrist said it was because we were not yet medicating his ODD. So, we decided to try Risperidone. This medication was specifically designed for defiance and would make him more compliant he said. The psychiatrist was right; it did. But at what cost… we would find out soon enough.

There were small things that other adults in our lives just didn't understand. Scott's way of communicating and understanding of how the world works was different than that of any other child. One time, he heard that the tooth fairy gave out money for lose teeth. So one day when Layla was in the jolly jumper and I was getting lunch ready he put his tooth in the middle of the springs and ripped his tooth out. It wasn't even lose. He was so focused on how to get money that the consequence didn't phase him even after he ripped it out.

Scott needed to be told things in different ways. I had to tell him how he should react because he had a lack of empathy. If he hit another child, he had absolutely no remorse. I had to explain to him how people 'usually act' when they feel bad. I had to teach him how to be fake in order for society to accept him and not fear him. I also had to explain things in a fearful way in order for him to understand or make changes. For an entire two years, he licked his lips repeatedly to the point where it hurt him to smile and the school teacher told me that the kids made fun of him all the time. People would say things like, "most kids get that during the winter," and recommend he use lip balm. I would have to explain that it wasn't that simple and that he gets bullied for it. Scott was so fixated on the behaviour and he wouldn't stop; the rash on his face from licking his lips was there year round. I told him that he would eventually lick his lips off and they would dissolve if he didn't stop it; I explained it was similar to how candies dissolve when you suck on them. That made him stop. Just like that. Then a teacher told him it wasn't true and it was unkind of his mom to tell him that. He made sure I knew the teacher thought I was being cruel. Therefore, the lip licking started up again. No one knew how to communicate to him in a way that he understood but me.

The psychiatrist prescribed Prozac for Scott because of it. At the age of six, he was on Concerta, Risperidone, Prozac and Melatonin. Drugged up, it was the only time he was never in trouble at school. He was doing very well ... because he was a complete zombie. It didn't feel right.... NOT AT ALL!

Scott developed an eye tick. Which, of course, Google said was a side effect from the most recent medication: Prozac. But the old-school doctor said it wasn't. I was determined to find a socially acceptable way to make the lip licking go away; there had to be a better way to address his anxiety. So, we stopped his medication, except for Concerta and Melatonin until we would find a better option, we returned to being lost in managing his anger and accepting the destruction in our home

Frustration

Once you start with the pediatrician, teachers, psychiatrists, government services or any support services, it's ridiculously confusing. They all act like experts, but you, the parent, are the "expert" on your child. They think their strategy is the best and only thing that works. They don't even collaborate within their own systems. It's disappointing as a client who truly needs their help.

It's not the individuals who work for those systems who are disappointing, it's the systems themselves that create the roadblocks in their thinking and ability to problem solve. In my experience, the system has been terrible at making sure families have enough support around them, so they actually feel strong enough to help their children. The doctors think it's medication, the psychologists, teachers, behaviour and attachment specialists all think the solution is behaviour modification in attempts to help and support families, but the reality is that you and your child are left feeling stuck in the middle as their guinea pigs. You are surrounded by experts and lose the ability to trust your own internal instincts once your child is labelled. I understand everything is trial and error, but the professionals also never consider the impact of their involvement along with the families' emotional management through acceptance of having a different life than the majority of other parents; the professionals tend to only operate on the health and safety perspective which is in itself cold and heartless feeling. I understand they are trying to help, but if they see any weakness from you, they worry about your ability to care for your child, and then, on the opposite end of the spectrum, if they see too much strength, they see someone who won't listen to them. I know this is a generalization, but I have been made to feel both while being caught in the system. As a professional within human services, I have sat in many of these meetings from the professional side, but now that I was on the receiving end of those services they have all made me feel like I was the reason Scott was having problems, from every eye roll, raised eyebrow, shared glare from professional to professional they made me feel judged that I wasn't able to manage it yet. I felt judged and isolated. It was bad enough we felt that way in our own community, we didn't need to feel that way when we were asking for help from professionals.

CHAPTER 15

EXHAUSTED

BESIDES USING MEDICATION, the only way I knew how to manage Scott was time-ins. I knew I wouldn't be able to do the time-ins forever; eventually Scott would be stronger than me and break out of my hold. It was difficult to hold onto him even now. I was meeting with my friend, Erin, a behavioural analyst. I had known that she worked with families who had children with autism and high needs, but I never considered that we fit into that category until she was talking about the scope of her field one day. I realized Scott would fit her child-specific programming. I decided it was time to be vulnerable with my best friend.

"Erin, I need to tell you something I am terrified to tell other people, even my family." I pressed on "Scott is…….. very violent to the point where he punches me, the walls and destroys anything and everything….I'm scared. It feels like he is intentionally trying to hurt me and I have no control in my parenting because I'm truly afraid of my son" Tears start to roll down my face while I continue to talk " I have no idea how to even help him or make it stop. He won't stay in the time out and time-ins won't work much longer."

How Many LabelsDoes One Child Need?

Erin moves in to hug me while I hold her. I feel better that I told her and her hug is warm and reassuring.

She whispers to me "Tara, you know you can always talk to me."

"I know, but I feel like just a terrible mother because of it. Like Scott deserves better than a mom who thinks this of him." I reply.

"You're not" she says "I can definitely give you some tools for tracking the reason why certain behaviours occur based on the event that happened right before and the consequence given."

She then went and grabbed tons of books for me to read and look through. She gave them to me and said "Also, if you truly think he is doing it intentionally it could be attention seeking and there is a sure way of seeing if it is for attention or not. You will need to find a place where you can contain him by locking the door. Make sure the room is empty so he can't hurt himself. If it is, in fact, attention-seeking behaviour, his violence will get worse for a period of time while you do this. But, one day, it will stop. He will test it again in the future, but you will know if he is in fact in control of his behaviour. Nothing about what she was saying felt right to me. It felt cold and heartless, but what else was I to do?

So, when the next meltdown occurred, I put him in his room, closed the door and held the doorknob. He screamed and screamed. He tried to fight against my hold on the doorknob. He thrust his fingers under the door while screaming in a high-pitched curdling cry that he would kill me. I no longer personalized it when he said that. He said it all the time. What bothered me was the scream. It sounded like he was possessed. My husband relieved me and we took turns holding the doorknob for more than half an hour. We questioned if this was normal.

Once Scott calmed down, we opened the door. He would lunge at us or scream the that he was not ready to "turn it around." We did this repeatedly for months. Just when we started to question if it was working, it got worse; but Erin had said it would get worse.

Just when I was ready to stop using this technique Scott punched and kicked the door so much that he cracked it. This had officially gone too far, but then there was no noise coming from his room anymore. When I opened the door, he was sitting quietly on the floor. He said "I turned it around mom, I'm ok now can I come out?." "If you think you're calm, then yes." I replied. That was the last time he ever punched, slapped or scratched Jack and I, so we rarely had to use that technique. Every once in a while I would use it, but it never lasted as long as it did in the past.

Was that it? Is that all it took? Was the violence finally over? It seemed too good to be true. Even though Scott was no longer hitting people, he targeted objects next. He had no idea how to channel his anger. It eventually led to him scratching his own arms and hurting himself. This battle was not over, but we were making progress.

Why didn't anyone tell me I could access someone like Erin? They thought medication was the only solution. They said to get a psychologist, but no one ever said there were people like Erin who actually helped with behaviours. The real problem was that you couldn't access professionals like her until a formal diagnosis was made and the child was labelled. ADHD is not considered by government standards to be a bad enough label to warrant access to individual financial support for parents, in order to access and be able to pay for professionals like Erin. When you are eligible, you have to know specialists or know of someone like Erin in order to access her.

CHAPTER 16

THE DARK SIDE

SCOTT PLAYED PRETTY rough with animals; it concerned me that he might be intentionally hurting them. I found a large number of dead cats on the acreage because Scott said he had trapped them, keeping them away from their mom and food. I pretended it wasn't intentional. When he stomped on the cat's tail, and did not move until it was in pain, I ignored it. When he showed no reaction to dead animals, I would tell myself he was too young to understand. But, when I saw him with a rope around our dog's neck, with blood coming from the dog's mouth while it was yelping for help, I could no longer pretend I wasn't worried, because it terrified me Jack and I never talked about it, so I can't say for sure what was going through his mind.

Being exposed to children with the combined diagnosis through my professional experience, made me aware that you need an entire team of health professionals to help kids like this. I had googled and found many different things that worked for kids with Oppositional Defiance Disorder. I had come to know that children his age do well in play therapy. So, I looked for a psychologist that used play therapy as a part of their assessment and treatment.

We sent the psychologist all of the information we had prior to the appointment. She was a well-known psychologist with amazing reviews, so we thought she would be the best to start working with our Scott. In her first sessions with Scott, she did play therapy. She had him lead the play and she assessed his decisions based on how well he played with her. He made sure she did what he asked her to do. He would give her a choice without a choice. She could only pick from two of the toys and he told her which weapons to use, and how she could use them to kill the other toys. We watched as he controlled the entire environment around her. It was so interesting to see his level of street smarts at such a young age. He was smart … in the wrong way. It terrified me. After reviewing the information we sent her and having one session with Scott, the psychologist told us he would end up with conduct disorder, which is what kids are diagnosed with when they are too young to be diagnosed with something more severe, something that predicts they will have antisocial personality disorder or become a psychopath. Instead, she diagnosed him with a neurodevelopmental disorder and sensory integration deficits. This would allow us to get him the help he needed now and hopefully prevent the diagnosis she suspected he would have as an adult.

Sadly, this felt right to me. I couldn't make sense of his behaviours and it felt like someone was finally listening to what was truly going on for him to make the right diagnosis. Although Erin had helped me see the behaviours, I felt like I needed the right diagnosis. I knew what he'd done was intentional and mean, but how could you say that about a young child? Who would want to be his friend now? We already struggled in isolation. How would I share the most recent events with family, my friends and still have them love and welcome him into their hearts? I looked over at Jack when she shared the information, and I could see the hurt in his eyes when she talked about the new diagnosis. But now what?

Scott's ADHD was still not properly medicated. I thought for sure we would have had this all figured out by now. Why was it just getting harder and harder? I knew in my heart there was a place in this world for everyone and there had to be an answer for Scott. Psychopaths and sociopaths can function well in society, and run successful companies. I needed to find a person who could be his psychologist and nurture his strengths to make him a successful adult that would be surrounded by people who loved and cared about him.

CHAPTER 17

BRAIN WAVES

I BECAME OBSESSED WITH googling different ways in which the brain worked and how to rewire it. I wasn't just searching for help anymore, I was searching for a cure. I needed to protect innocent animals and people from the man my son might become. I knew, with him being so young, there must be ways in which we could retrain the brain. I stumbled upon a local website that stated they did scientific assessments of the brain. It had some information about ADHD, and how it related to brain activity in children. The site stated they could reprogram the brain by creating new neural pathways with a computer program. They showed different ways that they could scan the brain to find out which areas needed extra support. It was called an electroencephalogram (EEG) test.

An EEG is a way to assess and record the way the brains cells communicate and operate through their natural electrical impulses. The EEG tracks the brain wave patterns and sends the signals to a computer that is able to record the results. It shows the valleys and peaks against a 'normal' brain pattern to see if there are any irregularities. Any irregularities may be a sign of seizures or other brain disorders.

Once I saw the image of a brain they had done, I needed to see inside my son's brain. I needed to understand my son's brain, so I booked an assessment. I thought this was a perfect first step in being able to see exactly what was going on in his brain. They told us to take him off of all of his medications for the assessment in order to get a true snapshot.

The exam was a few hours in length; Jack and I waited patiently for the results while Scott was in the testing room. The company who conducted the exam shared that they had never seen a seven-year-old's brain in such a state of anger and hyperactivity; they said there was no way even after tons of sessions, that they could help him. The help they could offer would only be minimal and he needed medication to help him—nothing else would help. I was blown away when I saw the image of his stressed brain. I had so much hope that this would work. I never thought the results would leave us feeling even more hopeless. It was the saddest thing to hear that my son was that angry and worried all of the time, but I wasn't giving up just yet.

CHAPTER 18

A WAY OUT

I FOUND A DIFFERENT psychologist in Calgary who worked with adults who had been diagnosed as a psychopath or sociopath. She referred me to another registered psychologist who conducted full assessments for children. Jack and I had a meeting with her and she shared that children with high-functioning autism can exhibit the same behaviours as conduct disorder. The clear difference is that one intends to cause harm and the other does not. She said Scott was too young for us to determine whether his actions were intentional or not. It was too early to tell if he would be a psycho- or sociopath. She completely disagreed with the previous psychologist.

I believed what he had done was intentional; We needed help and support. If the school, family and everyone else believed our son was not intentional with his hurtful actions, it would help them love him... like we loved him. I saw a high-functioning autism diagnosis for our son as a ray of hope versus people seeing him as a young psychopath or a sociopath. The label would allow him to continue as before, but be accepted by the community, his peers and everyone else, while we tried to find out how to help him. This was exactly what was needed. We knew if Scott had been diagnosed in a clinical setting at a hospital with tons of specialists round him he would never have gotten an autism diagnosis because he was intentional in what he did sometimes. I felt like we'd found a back-door solution to getting help because individual psychologists can also diagnose children and you don't need to go through a medical doctor necessarily. I was never really sure how Jack felt through this entire process. He never really shared anything with me.

The very next week, the psychologist did the full assessment on Scott and diagnosed him with Level One Autism. I was not expecting the level of support that even strangers would give us after that one diagnosis.

I truly felt the impact of that label when I had to run into the local small town fabric store for something. The second we got in there, Scott started flipping the light off and on and off and on. I knew if I told him to stop, he wouldn't. I would have to pick him up and leave ... but I only needed ONE thing. Tears were forming in my eyes while the women behind the counter glared at us. I knew if I said he had ADHD and ODD they would just say I needed to discipline him more because in my experience that's what the older generation feels about the diagnosis of ADHD. I felt so judged and ... hopeless. So, instead, I said, "He has level one autism which, in the new DSM, is the old Asperger's."

The women's faces instantly softened and the one elderly lady said, "Oh, darling... I will watch him while you grab what you need." I instantly cried so hard with gratitude while she came to me and held me in her arms while I wept. It was amazing to feel such a release and such a beautiful gesture from a complete stranger in a moment of stress.

I had to get fabric for my daughter's baby blanket since Scott had wrecked a part of it, and I never wanted one of my kids to feel second to the other one. Naturally, Scott made it virtually impossible for me to do anything for little Layla most of the time. I couldn't trust anyone to watch him; Being able to say what I'd said, changed how people looked at us. It changed my life. I finally felt like we were getting somewhere. Deep down, I knew it was all a lie and we directed the diagnosis and omitted certain details to work in our favour, but what else should we have done to feel supported and loved? Even though we helped lead the autism diagnosis because it's more socially acceptable, there were elements to Scott's behaviour that the psychologist solved for us. So, it always kept me guessing if Scott was intentional and in control of himself or not. Was it truly autism or was it a personality disorder like sociopath or psychopath?

CHAPTER 19

FALSE ACCEPTANCE

I SLOWLY STARTED TO realize that Scott did in fact think the same way as someone on the spectrum. Autism behaviours although can seem selfish and uncaring, are easily explained that they are truly impacted by their environment to the point that they don't intend on hurting anyone around them, but their struggles are far more severe. Even the slightest sound, change of schedule, bright light etc can cause a complete sensory overload that they meltdown and potentially hurt someone, etc. Scott had the same type of meltdowns as someone with high functioning autism. He was difficult if we had to change a schedule, he was highly demanding, he was hyper-focused at times, he would not notice another child in the room, etc. He had the same behaviours, but the only difference we saw, but never told the psychologist was that we believed Scott was intentional with his actions. However, the autism diagnosis helped us to understand him and the questions we needed to ask ourselves.

Scott, at age six, had digressed with his potty training. He was pooping in his underwear at school and home. He would try to get other kids to poop their pants, or take off their underwear. We had him checked by a doctor. It wasn't encopresis, an involuntary defecation, associated with emotional disturbances or psychiatric disorders. So, we resorted to the typical strategies for potty training once again. We tried bribing him with stars, stickers and candy. Nope. We tried to explain the natural consequence of losing friends. He would just say, "Well, if I stink and someone doesn't want to be my friend, then they aren't good enough friends." How do you argue with that logic? We even tried explaining what happens to your body when you feel a poop coming. Nothing, absolutely nothing, worked.

During a session with the psychologist, she said, "You have to find out what motivates him. What is he fixated on? Nothing else will matter more than that. If you use that as your bribe, he will listen to your direction."

Scott was obsessed with dinosaurs at that time. He knew every single one, and his favourite was the Carnatorous. So, I bought a pack of dinosaur cards with pictures and factual information on them. He got a card every time he went on the potty. Guess what? It worked instantly. Once he made his way through all of the cards, he was going on the toilet again. It was as if the diaper phase for a six year old had never happened.

The psychologist was an expert on Asperger's and was able to offer strategies that fit Scott's personality style. She directed us to the Asperger's experts' website. It was founded by an adult who had Asperger's, and was now teaching parents how to deal with kids like himself. He had an amazing diagram that helped me assess Scott's environment so we could see how to help him. The idea is that, if a meltdown is occurring, you need to assess the sensory input and change the environment before you ask them to do anything. The behaviour is a direct result of the sensory overload and you need to address that problem first.

With this mind-blowing information, I used this approach when Scott had his next meltdown.

He was screaming, hitting the back of the driver seat and jumping up and down refusing to do up his seatbelt; I had no idea why. When I looked around to the back seat, I realized the sensory input was different than every other day. We had someone else's dog in our vehicle because the neighbours asked me if I could drop their dog off for them at the vet and they would meet us there. He said he couldn't stand the dog being in the car. I gave him a piece of gum and told him it would help cover the smell of the dog. It worked!

I was starting to get into the groove, convincing myself that my son *did* in fact have autism. There was no way I could otherwise believe he would intentionally hurt animals, other children, and his parents. He was not in control of himself and his actions.

CHAPTER 20

IT'S TIME

I HAD SHARED THE assessment with the new diagnosis with the school, but it only made the teacher worry even more because she didn't have any extra school support. The Grade One schoolteacher, Mrs. Warner, was now starting to call me every night to share about how worried she was about Scott. It was starting to become a routine.

"Hello Tara, I am just calling to talk about how Scott took it too far in the classroom with another child again today. Yet again, he didnt take responsibility for his actions or feel bad about it when I talked to him about it either" She said.

"What exactly did he do this time Mrs Warner?" I would respond. She was an older teacher.

"Well today, he was slapping all of the kids butts and when they asked him to stop, he didn't." She explained.

"Ok, thank you. I will talk to him about it again tonight."

"Thank you. It's important that you keep talking to him about it, so he can change his behaviour." She would say in a stern voice.

"I understand. I am trying my best." I was so embarrassed

when she would call. I had no idea what to do I had talked to Scott now about it many times, but he would just say....

"What mom, all of the kids are doing it and they laugh."

My usual response would be "But, when they tell you to stop you need to stop because it means they don't like it anymore."

"But, they are laughing so that means they like it." He would reply.

I would get frustrated and try to explain it differently, but I could never get through to him on why slapping other kids butts was not ok because he never saw it as a bad thing.

This conversation would occur the same way every night and lasted for a few months. I could no longer be the only one helping him; I needed to have supports from people who specialize in Autism. Mrs Warner shared that the school had no extra supports for him even with his diagnosis, so there was nothing they could do to help him because they were a small town school. I know she cared about him, but I had no answers for her on what to do. When I would talk to Jack about it, he would just say that it wasn't a big deal "Kids will be kids." So, I stopped reaching out to him for support, and I decided it was time to take care of it myself, so I could step up and find the help he needed. I considered moving to a bigger town that had more supports for not only Scott, but for me as well.

Living on the acreage was wearing on my own self-care while feeling like I was alone in parenting. I decided it was time to have things in my life that would help me take care of myself. Like Yoga and Zumba, I enjoy relaxing and dancing. I needed to keep my own mental health in the forefront of trying to manage everything that was going on. I also desperately needed a school that could support Scott with his high level of needs; it was time to move closer to things for me and supports for Scott.

It's Time

Jack and I talked about how we had been struggling in our own relationship, and we decided it was best to move off the acreage and back into town. This would mean that Jack and I would live in separate homes. Without discussing how we felt, we both knew this was the start of the separation and it was only a matter of time before that conversation would happen between us. Neither of us were ready for that yet though.

Our place sold very fast and it was time to find a place in the new town. When we looked at places together, I said yes to a home that felt like Tara's home. I knew I didn't see Jack and I in that home, but it felt like the home for the kids and I. I had just taken a promotion at work in this new town, and this new beginning felt like the right thing to do.

The move went smooth, and Scott didn't even notice that Jack wasn't staying there during the weekdays. Jack worked in a different town for the majority of Scotts life thus far, so the move didn't impact Scotts relationship the way it was with his father at this point. The move was fast, seamless. I was also excited to see what I was able to do for my own mental health, so the very first thing I did after the move was settled was go to the nearest Yoga study to enroll in a class.

The Yoga study was such an amazing environment; It smelt calming and felt nurturing for my mind, body and soul, something I was in desperate need of. I was so excited for the kids and me in this new town in a new chapter. While I was at the counter looking at all of the classes, I was interrupted by this soft gentle voice speaking behind me.

"There are so many great choices in here it's hard to choose one hey." She said.

I turned around and responded, "There really is, I am new to town and I haven't been here before. Anything you would recommend?"

How Many Labels Does One Child Need?

"Oh hands down, Yin Yoga if you haven't tried it. It is so relaxing especially if you're a mom."

"I have two little ones, so I will look at that one for sure. My name is Tara." I reached out to shake her hand. She smiled and shook my hand back.

"My name is Sara and I am a new mom. I had little Ruby here just three weeks ago." She said picking up her carseat with a little sleeping baby in it.

"Awwww she is so cute. Yanno. I have my kids with me would you like to come back to my place for a tea or coffee. I just moved here and you would be my first visitor?"

"Sure, I didn't have any plans for this afternoon." Sara said with a smile. I gave her my address. We had hit it off right away. I was so happy. My heart was warm and I had just made my first friend in my new chapter.

I had no idea that I would quickly learn right after moving to this town that my son would ever intend to hurt poor little baby Ruby with his nerf gun. How could I ever think it was autism......He knew exactly what he was doing. The isolation had already started and I lost a potential friendship.

Our move to a new city was smooth because I planned the entire transition period out through the lens of autism. I made sure Scott had a perfectly lined out calendar of what we did each day before and after the move. There was nothing leading up to Sara and Ruby coming over that would have made me think Scott was having a rough day. I was completely blindsided by this weeks events.

I was shaken up; I couldn't believe I had to leave Layla asleep by herself in the house all alone while I worried that Scott was going to die. I wasn't able to be there to protect and take care of either one of them. It was just me... by myself. I tried to process the evening all night in between bouts of crying. *What had*

It's Time

I just seen? It's impossible for me to fall asleep tonight. I sneaked into his bedroom and looked over him. *He looked so peaceful. How could he just stop in the middle of running like he did and shoot Ruby like he did?* I moved through my tears into trying to problem solve how I was going to move forward with what I knew about him now.

He had been in control this entire time, always two moves ahead of me. He had played on my emotions by crying and convincing me he was a victim. He's not. He's one very smart little boy who knew how to manipulate human behaviour.

What he wasn't ready for, was a mom like me. I had been creating a false reality this entire time, believing he wasn't in control. It was a safe zone for me, a comfortable story that I believed for a short period. I could stay in denial about his cruelty for his entire childhood, but who would that help? I had to figure out the game, follow my own instincts and learn how to be in control of my home all by myself. It was time for me to see what his next move would be, so I could show him I that I had learned a few things, I am now his only opponent and I am ready to play. Your move, Scott.

PART TWO
CHECKMATE

CHAPTER 21

FOLLOWING MY INSTINCTS

I HAD JUST BOUGHT a bunch of hanging flowers for our yard. It was early spring, and every morning Scott and I would go out to water them. When I stepped onto the ladder to water one of the higher ones, I spotted three little eggs in a nest. I was so excited, I called Scott over. He was excited to see the eggs as well. So, every morning we would go and check on the eggs.

One morning, there were three little hatchlings. I was elated. So was Scott. We talked about them all day, every day. I loved that we were able to enjoy something together.

One week had passed, and we went to check on the birds. I looked up into the flower pot, and they were gone. I was so confused. I looked at Scott and he gave "that look." My heart sank. I asked him if he knew what had happened to the birds.

"I took care of them," he said.

I asked him what that meant.

He said, "Well, Mom, they bothered me so I put them in a tree, so their mom couldn't find them. It was an accident."

Knowing he was observing me and my next move, I had to be careful. Keeping a straight face, I asked him to show me where they were. He told me to follow him and we went to the tree in our backyard. He climbed into the tree and came out holding three dead baby birds.

"What happened to them" I asked

"I broke their necks and hid them to make sure their mom couldn't find them." He said with a smirk on his face.

"Oh." I said calmly. I was in complete shock, but I knew I needed to control my reaction before I figured out my next move. "Okay, well it's time to go to school, so go and get ready."

"Ok mom." He said " But, did you hear what I said, I said I broke their necks."

"I heard you, did you hear me I said get ready for school, its time to go."

He looked at me with a confused look and went inside to get ready for school. I walked him to the bus, dropped Layla off at daycare and then immediately called Jack. I could hear the disbelief in Jacks voice; this was something his heart couldn't handle. But my head was in the game. Jack quickly let me go off the call and said he was busy at work. I knew exactly how I was going to handle this. I was going to talk to my son…the real version, the shadow side, of my son. The dark one, the one I did not want to accept. I had to unearth the reality of what was happening. I was ready to make my move. He would never see it coming.

I picked him up from school. I told him we were going for a walk alone before picking up his sister. While we were walking, I said, "Scott, I think you meant to kill the birds. I don't think it was an accident. You are smarter than that. I think you did it because you didn't like that I was paying attention to the birds, so you made sure to kill them."

He stopped in his tracks and said, "Mom, that's the first time you have ever been able to read my brain."

He held my hand after I said it. He'd never done that. We walked, hand in hand, like it was the beginning of a new relationship.

From that day on, he knew I had learned the game, and was now a worthy opponent. Although I was mortified, I was never going to show weakness or let him manipulate me again. I needed to know exactly what I was working with. How far was he willing to take this extreme behaviour and could it be fixed? I refused to be a mother who visited her son in prison, so I dedicated myself to finding out how to beat him at his own game.

Now that I understood his motivation and perspective, I was determined to come up with a program to encourage and discipline his unwanted behaviours while listening to his needs and letting him have some control. One of the group homes I worked with through Tracy Cook with Cook Counseling had a great system called Children Helping Improve Parenting Success (CHIPS). I'd found out all about the program while working with the home, I decided to start using it with Scott. He was seven years old now; it was worth a try.

CHAPTER 22

TICKS AND TOKENS

I CALLED IT THE Ticks and Tokens program and it changed our lives. The Parenting Program that Tracy Cook Developed has an element of consequences, but a large amount is positive reinforcement.

TICKS- consequences. For example, whenever Scott would hit someone, he automatically lost all of his daily privileges.

If he got six ticks in a day, he would get an X and lose all of his privileges—no TV, no sugar, and an early bedtime. If the school ever called me, it was an automatic X for that day.

Since there are seven days in a week there is the potential for seven X's. One a day. So there are seven levels and at the end of the week we would determine which level of privileges he would have for the next week. For example, If he got no X's, he would be on a level seven. Level seven included all of the privileges from the other levels PLUS he got to spend his tokens and have a playdate. If he got one X, then starting Friday night he was on level six for the following week. Which meant he could not spend his tokens or have a playdate. If he got two X's for the week, he would be on level five. Which meant he could not have any technology for the entire week except one night on the weekend and one night on the weekday. And so on and so on. Since he now knew the consequences, this brought him comfort. He loved knowing the program. This showed him that it wasn't my control or his, but that it was the rule and he was in control of his level. It brought him comfort, and it wasn't a power struggle. I was just following the rules. He tested me all the time in the beginning. I made sure I provided an insane number of tokens for positive things during this time. It was hard to find the positives when he was losing his privileges on a daily basis

TOKENS- positive reinforcement

The trick though is to make sure you balance the ticks with a HUGE amount of tokens. The tokens motivated him to want to make better choices. It was a constant reinforcement of encouraging positive replacements for behaviour. Even if a day was a tough day, I still needed to find things to token him on. For example, on the days he hit the wall instead of me, I would give him one hundred tokens along with losing his daily privileges (An X). He became curious about the purpose of the tokens. I told him they were like money: he could buy things with them. We sat down and wrote out what he could buy his with tokens. He also had to save twenty percent of earned tokens to save up for some bigger ticket items.

Go Kart—66,000 tokens

Fish—1000 tokens

XBox—1000 tokens

TV in his room—800 tokens

Fishing rod—400 tokens

Sleepover on the weekend—60 tokens

10-20-dollar toy, cash or game—30 tokens (he used this one every time he was on a level seven)

I printed it off so he could see it on the fridge. It wasn't long before I realized I was not even ticking him for hitting; all he was getting were tokens. It was amazing. He was on level seven for months because he understood the consequences and knew how many ticks it took to lose things. He took it seriously. I could now move to the problems that I'd never addressed before, like him not doing what I asked him to do when I told him to do something. I was now able to tick those things. I slowly addressed one problem behaviour at a time. I made sure to warn him about what he would get ticked on; I changed the program gradually, but always informed him of the changes before I implemented them. Lying, stealing and hitting, which were once only ticks, were now automatic X's because he rarely did those things anymore.

We still run this system today. I have given him tokens for being kind and now everyone says I have the kindest boy. He was never like that before. He knows the level system. He runs to do what I asked him to do now to avoid getting a tick. It's the most amazing system that keeps me calm because I can just tick, tick, tick, tick, tick then it's an X. It makes me a better parent. And now my daughter knows X's are "bad," so when I say she would get an X, she cries. She doesn't even understand it, but she knows it is not good. I need to keep telling myself that the tokens matter more than the ticks or X's so, I am just starting to give her tokens for her positive behaviours. It's a positive reinforcement on a developing brain, even though we just expect kids to behave that way. The thing that I have to make sure is, if I have given Scott an X, I need to cancel our plans for that day. I need to stay very strict.

One day, I didn't, and the very next day, he pushed the X off like it was nothing. It took me an entire two weeks to reinforce the program again. Never again. I learnt the hard way. I even got ice cream with my daughter and didn't give Scott any just to show how serious I was. I know it sounds cruel, but the reality is my son is smart and manipulative. Being strict with the program and following through on my word is the environment he thrives in. He is a completely different kid now. To the point where Jack said, "See, I told you he just needed to mature." I didn't bother arguing with him on where Scott's success was coming from because I knew the truth.

CHAPTER 23

STATISTIC

THE TICKS AND Tokens program was working and I had needed to be consistent with it. Jack wasn't able to be consistent. Jack would spend weekends with us and one night, Jack got Scott excited right before bed. He put a blanket on the floor and put Scott and Layla on the blanket and pulled it for a fun ride. They both loved it. He did it a few times and then, he said, "This is the last time now." However, when he finished that turn, they asked for more. With typical children, you can give them one more without consequence. Not with Scott. My husband caved, gave them one more ride, and then stopped. My daughter's response was typical. She cried and kept asking for more. The second he said "No" in a stern voice, she stopped asking. Scott, on the other hand, hounded him then started punching his dad in the chest. I told Jack it was because he hadn't stuck to his word. Scott would have been fine if his dad had stopped when he had said he would, but, because he gave them one more ride, it confused Scott.

Through the whole process of raising a difficult child, Jack and I grew apart. I had been obsessed with getting help, answers and support, and we lost the simplicity in our relationship. We had marital struggles aside from the difficulties with Scott. When Scott showed to be more and more difficult, Jack stepped back, knowing I would get Scott the help he needed. After the night, settled and the kids were in bed, I sat on the kitchen floor crying. Jack sat next to me and said, "I know it might not seem like this, but I know you are trying and doing what's best for Scott. I don't tell you that enough, I'm sorry I can't be the one to help, but thank you for all that you do." He held me while I cried, but in my heart, I knew our relationship was over. I had done everything up until this point feeling so alone and I could no longer trust him to be there for me.

Scott was my priority. Scott was also Jack's priority, but in a different way. The softest of the men around Scott was Jack. Jack is kind, gentle and a joker, but not able to remain consistent with discipline. I had accepted that Scott was difficult, but Jack just wanted things to be easy and smooth. That's what most people want. Granted, I can't imagine I was very easy to deal with during this process for Jack either. I know some would say the struggles we had in our marriage could be environmental to what was also going on for Scott. And that could be true too. Some think its food, which could also be true. It could have been his difficult birth; it could be genetics; it could also be a combination of all of those. The reality is, we will never know. I am sure psychologists could have a filed day with trying to diagnose him based on what I have shared, but the bottom line is that Scott's behaviours are what we had to identify and manage. The diagnosis was merely a label.

I used the labels and diagnoses only to learn and grow while being stuck in the how this happened and why did it happen. My intention wasn't to label my son, but more to understand "who" my son was. If I'm being honest, I was relieved when

Statistic

Jack stepped back from us during the journey, or maybe I pushed him away.

Scott was helping me grow through this. They say that people who have children with disabilities it increases their chances for divorce, and we fell into that statistic. We suffered in silence and isolation from each other and our extended families. This led to more and more arguments, which led to Jack working away more and more. We decided to officially separate.

Scott, as a seven-year-old boy, struggled with the news, but we made sure to tell him together. Since Jack already worked away, lived in a different city, and home altogether nothing really changed, so it was not a huge impact to Scott's daily life. Layla was too young, so it didn't phase her at all. We both agreed I was to be the full-time parent. Before Jack left the house that day, he said "In the event we ever worry about Scott hurting Layla we would need to talk about separating them." Instantly I felt sad having to choose which child to stay with me. I replied," I don't think we will encounter that and I will try my hardest to not have to separate them as siblings." We both agreed that it was better if they were kept together, but there was an element of a possibility we may need to discuss that in the future. I was determined that it wouldn't come to that. With that Jack left the house. He still saw the kids most weekends because him having time with the kids was not only his right, but we both felt it was very important. Jack loves his children, there is no question about that. We were completely amicable, and we made sure to reduce the impact to the children. Scott was adjusting very well to the change because of the efforts we both made as parents.

I finally felt like I could breathe. Although I felt supported by my closest friends and stepmom, I was ultimately alone with my parenting struggle. I was more than okay with being alone in it. It wasn't as scary knowing what to expect. I was trying my hardest to avoid the worst when the most amazing thing happened. We went to watch my niece dance and there was a girl there who was doing a solo; she cried the entire time on stage. She danced as a tribute to her brother who had committed suicide the previous year. It was a powerful performance. I looked over to see that Scott was starting to tear up. This was the first time I had seen him show emotion, but this was also the very first time he has ever seen anything so deep and dramatic. He connected with it. I went to wrap my arms around him when, all of a sudden, his sister started rubbing his arms with her hands while looking into his eyes with love. I no longer felt alone. Layla, at two years old, was able to express her love for her brother just the way he was. I cried for our little family, knowing we were going to be okay because, even if the worst ever happened, we would go through it together. Whether I wanted her to be or not, she was "all in" because she loved her brother. I was filled with love and peace. I thought we could make it through anything, until I realized a sliver of my fear would always linger in the back of my mind.

CHAPTER 24

ALTERNATIVE MEASURES

THERE WAS A lot of media coverage during this time about the benefits to CBD(Cannabidol) oil. I was unsure about using it for children. It wasn't until I started talking to a few of my friends who were using CBD oil to help with their own pain and anxiety, that I started to consider it. I didn't want the side effects of pharmaceuticals; I needed a better way to managing Scott's behaviour. My friend suggested I meet with a particular doctor just to ask questions, so I made the appointment. When I told the doctor about Scott's behaviour, he said Scott could definitely benefit from CBD oil. So, why not. Let's try it.

I didn't tell the school or the daycare because I feared their judgment. After two weeks of daily use, I asked the school and daycare if they noticed anything different. Scott's teacher said he was "more calm and focused" in class. The daycare worker said he didn't try to force his game on the other kids, so that he was "more calm and focused" than usual. Had they really just said the EXACT same thing? That's insane that it had impacted him that much. I thought for sure this was the solution and all he needed was the ADHD medication and CBD oil and he would be perfectly fine. So, I felt more confident taking him out shopping when I needed to.

Things were going so well. Or so I thought. We went into a shoe store because Scott needed a new pair of shoes for school. He put on a pair of shoes that were not appropriate for school. I told him we could not buy those shoes. He yelled, "No! I want them!" and started running around the store in the shoes. I finally caught him and told him to take them off. He took them off and put on his boots. *Phew, he listened to me.* Then all of a sudden, he yelled, "I'm stupid, Mom, and I might as well kill myself." He ran right out the door and into the busy parking lot in the dark. I ran after him, leaving my daughter in the store. I grabbed him right before he got hit by a truck. He refused to come with me and told me that he wanted to kill himself. I put him in our vehicle, went back into the store to fetch my daughter and we left.

I tried to hold back the tears, but I cried all night. During these moments of absolute despair, I would call my stepmom to just cry. Although she was far away, she was always there for me.

Maybe Scott should be a medicated zombie. At least then he would be safe. He should be calm and able to handle situations with the ADHD meds and CBD oil, but they didn't seem to be working. He started to hate the taste of the CBD oil, so I stopped administering it to him since we hadn't seen enough of a benefit anyway. He may have been more calm and focused, but not to the degree that the oil would be the only type of medication that we needed to use if he was running into the streets still. We needed a better solution while we were still working out the ticks and tokens program.

CHAPTER 25

THE TRUTH

KNOWING MY SON was someone western culture and medicine did not yet understand, I moved away from medications and allopathic practices and searched out other forms of help. I kept him on the medication while I sourced out other forms to help him with the hope of weaning him off of his pharmaceutical medication. I started to talk with my girlfriends more about spirituality. Heather, shared that her favoured form of therapy was Body Talk. She told me how healing it was for her.

Body Talk is based on the idea that our body has three brains, and holds past life information. We hold it in our chakras and, when our body is out of energetic alignment, it will manifest as emotional distress, behaviours and physical ailments. Our head, brain and thoughts aren't necessarily even our own. Our thoughts are developed through our childhood and our parents and society impact how we think. We may think our thoughts are our own, but the brain is so much more complicated than we can even begin to understand. The idea is that we don't listen to our other two brains as well (gut brain and heart brain) or even integrate what they are also trying to communicate to us; we fail to follow our gut instincts in our very primal make-up. The gut brain are those internal gut feelings that sometimes our heads convince us out of doing. Most people know the difference between those two, but we forget we have a heart brain as well. It centers us around the right decision, love and how we are affected and impacted. Sometimes we neglect our own heart for the sake of thinking our head is making the right decision for us. Bodytalk as the form of therapy is working on the alignment of all three.

I had just started to expand my interest and curiosity with my own spirituality, starting with yoga practices. It was grounding for me. I felt more at peace and ready to help my son when my mind, body and soul were all doing well. The reality was, I wasn't doing well. The journey through all of this was devastating. I was not only searching for help, but answers and a reason why. I had shared with Erin and Heather what was going on for me, but I had not once shared how alone, terrified and scared I truly was. I was still protecting him and our family, but sacrificing myself. I knew the two people who loved and cared about me as my kindred soul sisters were Erin and Heather. So, if either of them gave me advice I trusted them enough to blindly follow their direction, so I reached out to the Body Talk practitioner Heather said wasn't her regular practitioner, but the one she felt was very powerful in distance work. Allison Bachmeier from Calgary Alberta.

I shared minimal details about my son with Allison. She said she would do a session with him. By now, I had tried all of the western medicine options available to me and spent thousands of dollars, so what was the harm in another hundred dollars for one Body Talk session? She required a recent photo of Scott's face and suggested taking one tonight when I got home. So, I went home that night I asked Scott if I could take a picture of him. He refused, which was odd. Usually he could care less. He said, "I don't want that woman to have my picture." I was shocked. He followed up by saying, "I know there is a woman you are going to give it to and she can't have my picture."

I'd had my phone call with the practitioner, Allison, while I'd been at work and I never mentioned Body Talk at all in front of Scott. How could he possibly know? I responded, "I don't know what you're talking about, I just want your picture."

So he yelled in my face, "NO!" Then he punched me and started screaming and breaking things. It had been so long since he had hit me. I told him if he couldn't get control of himself, he would lose things out of his room. He grabbed a hanger and hit me with it. I started grabbing his toys and books and taking them out of his room. He kept hitting me and yelling. I kept going and, before I took his hockey trophies, he stopped. In utter despair... he sat on his bed and said he needed to be alone. I left him alone.

About thirty minutes later, he called me back to his room. With a defeated look on his face, he said, "She can have my photo now ... just like me ... like I am right now." Goosebumps ran down my spine ... and I took the photo.

The Body Talk practitioner did the session on Scott the next day over the phone. I was his surrogate. I listened to her work on him through me. At one point, she started to energetically pull things out. I cringed and thought ...*PLEASE stop hurting him.* She instantly stopped and said, "For some reason, I can't do this with you; I need to do this part alone." She left the call.

When she came back on the call, she shared that the two past lives he holds are very traumatic ones. One was as a survivor of the holocaust who had been kept alive only to endure daily torture ... until the end of his life. The other was as one of Hitler's men, who enjoyed torturing others. This man also lost his entire family to a house fire. Everything and everyone he loved had died in a house fire. She recommended doing more sessions of bodytalk, but she said she moved and did some work within the session. I had no idea what that all meant, but she also said to do smudging with Scott after the session. I cried to think of my son as a tortured soul. The Body Talk session certainly changed the way I looked at him.

That night, when I got home, there was a note from the teacher in Scott's backpack. He had hurt another child at school. When I started to ask Scott about it and explain that he would be getting an X, he punched me on the arm and ran to his room. I started my punishment routine of pulling his stuff out of his room. I would carry one thing out at a time and not stop until he behaved or until he had nothing left in his room. This time was the worst it had ever been. He broke his baby plaques and destroyed his favourite teddy bear, but I kept taking things out. He was screaming and, when I reached for things, he bit my forearm. Shaking, I finally let go of his grip when he grabbed a hanger and hit me on the head with it. I needed him to stop. Otherwise, he would keep breaking his own stuff, hurt himself and me, and it wouldn't end.

So, I kept going. I carried his dresser out of his room; I carried his bed, then his bed frame. All that was left was a blanket and a pillow. Everything was stuffed in the hallway. Right before I was going to hold the door closed with him in there alone, he broke into tears. "Okay, Mom. I'm okay now." I responded " You get 100 tokens for deciding to turn it around. I will give you your own time." I left him alone for about thirty minutes before I came back into his room to check on him.

Both of us were exhausted and sad. He was laying in the middle of the room on the floor, so I laid next to him and we both looked up at the ceiling. I thought about what the Body

The Truth

Talk lady had said about this little soul being tortured. I thought about all the other things I learned from other professionals and teachers. It wouldn't hurt to see him through a different lens. I said, "You know, Scott, I don't know what happened to you in the past, or what you have been through, but I need you to know that NO MATTER WHAT, I will never leave you; I will ALWAYS be here for you."

And for the first time, when Scott looked at me, he actually made eye contact. Then he snuggled into me. That was the last time I ever had to take stuff out of his room. From then on, my mission was to search for other means to help him through this journey in life. I had to make a difference because by age twelve, or so, he would be big enough to do what he wanted. I still had an influence on his development until then. I knew I could do it.

CHAPTER 26

CREATE SPACE

INSTINCTUALLY I THOUGHT, maybe it would help to develop a nightly ceremony to connect to my son and ask for help from our higher selves, elders, God or whatever was out there. Let's face it, I had absolutely no idea what I was doing. I had learned the basics of how to smudge from a mandatory Indigenous Training I had taken at work, but I had never incorporated that, or any type of ceremony, into my home and daily life. At first, Scott made fun of smudging. Especially when I made him close his eyes while I smudged his eyes to see the truth, his ears to listen to the messages he needed to hear, his mouth to speak with kindness, protection for his whole body, and his heart to feel compassion. It was a very focused, raw, real and serious ritual, especially for a seven-year-old. He would close his eyes, but smirk while I did it. I knew if I stayed focused, he would eventually start to feel it.

After a few nights of smudging, he started to cry afterwards—the paralyzing type of cry where real heavy tears flow. Scott had never cried like that. Scott was always so standoffish and never talked about his day or his feelings. Through his tears, he told me about how he was bullied because he licks his lips. I knew he was bullied before, but only because the teachers told me. He never once mentioned it to me. I was shocked; he was crying, sharing how his heart was seriously wounded. He didn't punch anything, he just cried. I told him it's okay to cry. I held him while he cried himself to sleep that night.

Our nightly routine now included Scotty's water works of tears after the smudging. I had opened a new door, but I had no way of knowing when the crying would stop. The cleansing and release was working well, but what else could I do to help him through it all?

I knew through my own yoga practices that meditation also helped with anxiety, healing and growth. So, I googled different meditations for children. I landed on a YouTube site called Horizons; it was a kids' meditation channel that had an older woman's voice with an accent. Scott instantly gravitated toward this woman's voice and he loved it. We would smudge, cry, talk about our day, and then I would snuggle right beside him while we did the meditation. He loved it when I held him after his release of tears. It was beautiful. My son no longer repelled my affection. We would fall asleep on the floor, and we did this every single night. He would talk during the entire meditation, but then he started to talk about what visions we had while listening to the meditation.

One day, he started sharing what his dreams were about. He had never talked about any dreams before. Finally, in his despair, he shared that he always dreamed about me dying. He shared the specifics of one where both of us were stuck in a cage above a field of zombies. He never watched any zombie shows, how could he even know what they were? He said there was someone flying around and selling wings. He bought a pair for each of us. He put a pair on me first to save me and he let me go to fly away to safety; instead, I started to fall. As I was falling, he realized my wings were cardboard and his were metal. Only he would survive. He hadn't meant to kill me. He said that I was always dying, sometimes from attacks by sharks or other animals. He didn't understand why. He cried when he told me.

I held him because it was the only thing I could think to do. Then he asked if he could sleep with me at night because his nightmares were too scary. I wondered if this was an intentional move, a way to manipulate me. The outcome of having him in my bed at night was love and connection between us. It was worth letting my guard down and loving him the way I knew how. My stepmom had taught me to unconditionally love your child regardless of what they have done to you. You are their only mother, and you have to sit in a beautiful, guilt free, unconditional love regardless of what they have done. I was a mother who loved her child unconditionally regardless of how mean he was to me. But of course, I still kept my guard up for the possibility that he was making a chess move to see if I would cave based on him now using his tears to manipulate me.

Now, I finally understood what was happening with him. Most kids that age don't ask to be back into their parents' bed, but he wasn't going to stay in my bed forever. And now, I had a different perspective of who he was. The idea of a family bed wasn't a terrible idea, so I let him sleep back in my bed. He had started to show other emotions besides anger and frustration, he was ready to grow and evolve. Everyone said he would grow out of his lack of empathy, aggression and energy, but it took work. Work to nurture that part of him and his depth in spirituality. We were nowhere near being "okay" just yet. I was just starting to learn about who he truly was.

CHAPTER 27

HIGHER PURPOSE

IT WAS HALLOWEEN and a young boy came to the door as Batman. When he left, Scott told me that the boy was unhappy and Scott wanted to know why. I asked him how he knew he was unhappy.

"I just know." He said.

He talked about the young boy all night. He asked me tons of questions: "Do you think his parents love him? Do you think they take care of him? Do you think he has friends?" and on and on.

I had to reassure him by making up a lie that the boy was at home happy with his parents, but who was I kidding? If my son was worried, there must be something wrong because over forty kids came to the door tonight and this was the only child he was worried about. I realized maybe my son is an empath, with a paranormal ability to feel the emotional states of others. Perhaps his struggles at school had to do with the impact of having many kids, with all their chaotic energy, around him. Being so young, Scott wouldn't understand what was going on or have the ability to protect himself, so he reacted.

I read up on all of the different types of empaths. I came across article after article that went into a detailed description of "Indigo children" on Wikipedia.

Indigo children are children that are sent to this earth during this time to challenge our societal norms and change how we look at things. I realized my son did that all the time. The indicators of an indigo child are that they are:

empathetic, curious and strong-willed; possess a clear sense of self-definition and purpose; show a strong innate subconscious spirituality from early childhood (which, however, does not necessarily imply a direct interest in spiritual or religious areas); have a strong feeling of entitlement, or deserving to be here; high intelligence quotient; inherent intuitive ability; resistance to rigid, control-based paradigms of authority; they may function poorly in conventional schools due to their rigid authority, their being smarter or more spiritually more mature than their teachers, and their lack of response to guilt, fear or manipulation-based discipline.

It's noted that many children in this category get ADHD and or Autism diagnoses as well or there is controversy that it falls on potentially being illness, poor or narcissistic parenting.

Obviously, there is a disconnect between the medical and the spiritual world. When you consider mind, body, soul as all being important for our mental health, the medical field has neglected the soul part of humans because no one knows without a doubt what exists. This makes it difficult to consider spirituality in looking at mental illnesses, diagnosis, etc. Instead of allowing those who are gifted to use their perspective in helping human kind we may tend to medicate some of those humans and miss out on seeing from a different side. Science is evidence. Spirituality's evidence changes from human to human. As much as people sometimes can see how science and spirituality relate,

Higher Purpose

I now completely see how it's not about them relating, but that one cannot exist without the other. Thanks to being blessed with an Indigo child with ADHD and past life trauma.

I was convinced my son was an Indigo child. There was so much more for me to learn in order to parent this amazing being. But more importantly, I could fall in love with who he was again. I believed in what he stood for instead of labelling him according to societal "norms." Now, I was thirsty to learn more with him and more about him as we make moves towards a holistic lens into solution-focused, problem-solving life. There was hope; there is always hope.

CHAPTER 28

NEW LENS

AFTER REALIZING MY son had a greater spiritual understanding than I did, I located an energy protection oil for empaths through my friend Heather, who had taken some courses through Kim. Kim Wuirch, who created Employed by Angels, had developed the protection oil for empaths. I thought, well I should just order it and not tell Scott what it is. Just see what happens. So, that's what I did.

The first day I put it on him, I told him I was just trying it on him. He was used to trying different types of medication, so he didn't ask any questions about it. The next morning while he was getting ready for school he asked " Hey mom, yanno that stuff you put on my wrists yesterday. Can I have it on again?"

Curious I asked, "why do you want it on again?"

"Because, yesterday I made ten-out-of-ten star decisions and usually I make two-out-of-ten star decisions." He said.

"Is that star thing something from school?" I asked curiously.

He seemed annoyed that I didn't understand. "No. I just know it's that many stars type of a day."

"What does a two-star day look like?" I pressed on so curious about where the star thing came from.

"On normal days, I always ask the kids whose parents didn't pack them very much food in their lunches to play. I feel bad for them." He expanded. "On those days, I end up making decisions from my dark red energy and getting into trouble with them because they like doing the bad things with me. I am the brain in the bad things we do if I have those people with me."

I asked "what made you not play with those kids today?"

"I didn't feel bad for them today, and at recess I played the way I wanted to play and it didn't get me into trouble, so can I please have some more on today?"

From this day on, I realized my advocacy for Scott would shift. Instead of hearing what professsionals say and following their advice at every turn, I would turn the table and become more curious and ask more questions because, guaranteed, there would be a different reason why Scott made the choices he made. I also realized that the school doesn't ask good questions, they just assume the worst.

My first chance to test this new tactic was when I was called to the school because Scott put glue on the slide. He was expected to write an apology. But, he was mad at the teachers and refused. He kept yelling that he hadn't done anything wrong. Instead of me just agreeing with the school, I asked him questions in front of the teacher I said, "Scott, why did you do it?"

He said, "Because all of the kids at recess walk up the slide, and I thought it would help our shoes stick so we could run up the slide faster."

Wow. "Well, that's really inventive of you and a good way to solve a problem. But the school has a rule about going up the slide to prevent kids from getting hurt. If kids are walking up then the kids who slide down would run into them."

"But I don't understand why it's a rule if no one slides down it, Mom. It's not used for that anymore. Why can't we use it in a different way? If that's how kids like to use it? "It's for kids and not adults so why can't we decide how we want to use it?"

I was struggling with dismissing his rationale but it was a valid answer. I knew the school wouldn't overturn the rule. They wanted him to see how his decision wasn't safe for everyone. I thought about it … and said, "I agree with you completely, Scott, but you know what? Maybe on weekends, moms take their younger kids to the park and they might slide down it. So, even though you don't see it, doesn't mean it doesn't happen. Younger kids still use the slide that way. What if a child got stuck to the slide because of your glue?"

Scott's face relaxed and he said, "That makes sense, Mom. I won't do it again." Then he apologized to the principal.

An Indigo child needs answers that make sense before they can understand. They challenge the norms if they can't make sense of something. If I couldn't find an answer, and explain why we did what we did, I would have to change my rules. I'd have to advocate for him, to help change the rules that no longer made sense. It was enlightening to start looking at all the rules that affect us and ask if they still held. Before I understood what he needed in order to make sense of our world, he needed to discuss it. In the past, that incident would have led to a complete meltdown at home because he would not accept accountability, get frustrated, and use his anger as a form of communication. He needed adult explanations. Moment by moment, I was falling in love with my son's mind, soul, energy and bigger purpose.

It was late November when the school's principal called "Tara, Scott brought a knife into the school and he is being suspended could you come and get him immediately please?"

"Oh of course" I responded. "I am on my way."

When I arrived, Scott was sitting with the teacher. She said goodbye to Scott without looking like she wanted to talk to me.

I stopped her and said" Hi, sorry can you just review the situation with me more please. What did Scott do exactly?"

"Well" she said" He brought a knife into the school and told another one of the students that he was going to murder the elf of a shelf!"

Instead of worrying as I would typically do, I said "Oh, what kind of knife did he bring in?"

"A butter knife, but regardless of what kind, the school's policies are no weapons brought to school."

"Oh I completely agree and understand. He will be getting an X for doing this which means he loses all of his daily privileges, but in hopes of helping him learn what was wrong in this did you ask him why he did it?"

"No, I didn't ask him." She realized. So, I looked at Scott and said, "Scott, why would you want to murder the "elf on the shelf?" With a serious look on his face he replied, Mrs. Jeannie loves to keep a very clean classroom. And every night this "thing" comes to life, messes up her classroom, and touches everyone's things and I thought she would be happy when I would murder him so he couldn't do that to her or my things anymore."

The teacher looked shocked. Scott was doing it out of kindness and care for her. I proceeded.

"Scott. What do you think your friends would think about it?"

"Well, I know they would be scared when they saw all of the blood." He said

"Why didn't you just tell Mrs. Jeannie how you felt about the elf on a shelf?" I asked.

"When a kid is bullied at school, and we tell a teacher, it

New Lens

never makes it stop. Telling a teacher never solves anything." He responded confidently.

"Oh, I said back." I looked at Mrs. Jeannie hoping she would have something to say at this point. She was in such disbelief that she had nothing to say. Honestly, I was stuck as well.

"Scott, whenever you feel that way you need to tell Mrs. Jeannie instead of taking it into your own hands. Because Scott, the elf on a shelf isn't real and its Mrs. Jeannie who messes up the room."

He looked up at her with a confused look on his face and asked her "Mrs. Jeannie why do you make me clean up my mess, but then you make a mess and you laugh at it?" "Why don't you laugh at my messes then?"

She kneeled down at this point to look him directly in the eyes and said, "I am so sorry Scott, I had no idea that you felt that way. The elf on a shelf is a game I play and it makes everyone laugh. It was supposed to be a secret that I am in charge of that game, but now that you know can you be my helper?"

His face lit up "Yes!" He said

"But remember Scott, we still need to keep our messes clean and its only when we use the elf that the mess will be funny." She said while winking at him

"Of course Mrs. Jeannie. I understand now. I am sorry if I scared you"

"That's ok Scott. I will see you back here in a couple of days." She replied, "Scott, do you mind waiting over there while I talk to your mom for a second?"

"Of course." He replied.

"Tara, I am so sorry I didn't realize that was why he brought in the knife." She said. "Thank you for showing me why he did it."

"You're welcome, I have learned the hard way how to see

things from his perspective, but I now know that I have to remain curious with him, and ask the questions that help me see how he thinks in order to ultimately how truly amazing he is." I responded. "Have a great rest of your day." And I took Scott home for his in-school suspension. But this time, he didn't blame anyone else, he was sorry for what he had done and wrote his teacher an apology letter. He also didn't argue or get mad when he had an X because he knew it was for a good reason.

CHAPTER 29

BALANCE

EVERYTHING WAS FEELING so much better in Scott and I's relationship. Then one day, I found my bras and panties underneath Scott's bed. Once again, I was filled with terror. It had been a year since I had been this terrified. The first thing that ran through my mind was worry about him wanting control, and the potential diagnosis this kind of behaviour could receive. I asked him why he had my underwear. He said he didn't know why.

I found them there every day and he could never explain his actions to me. My fear of what he could become reared its ugly head. Since I had seen the benefit that Bodytalk did for my son, I decided to also get the same help for myself. Heather recommended a woman that she used and was going to her on a monthly basis. Her name was, Ashley Rowland-Moellenbeck, creator of Soul Movement, and during one session I brought up the topic of my son.

"I know we are working on my own things, but I feel like I want to share with you that my son, Scott, is starting to take my bras and panties and hide them in his room. I am wondering if maybe you have a different perspective on that than what the medical field would say about him."

"Well, she said checking in with me and the spiritual world. Its interesting what is coming up, but since you have been attracted to the moon a lot lately and the moon is a feminine planet, you are craving to connect to your feminine side. Maybe just maybe, he is asking for the same thing as well?" She said. Blown away of the possibility of Scott screaming for me to be more feminine and not a psychopathic tendency I was curious to see if I could change his behaviour by nurturing that side of myself. I was definitely holding more of a strict drill sergeant parental role, and Scott had been responding to it in a positive manner. I was willing to give it a try. What did I have to lose?

I went home and became softer, but still strict; I worked at balancing the two masculine and feminine energies. I gave lots of hugs and made sure to do a mediation with my son that night so we could snuggle. The next day, there was no lingerie under Scott's bed. Was that truly all he needed? This boy keeps astonishing me with how well he is connected to the energy balance in our home and within me.

I found it difficult to manage my level of softness; how much softness was too much? I was always on my toes, assessing what to do in each situation and moment. Scott walked up to me randomly one day and stomped as hard as he could on my toes while staring me down. It was a control tactic that I had to be on top of. I never made a face or a sound. I just stared him down and gave him an X for the day. That was an example of something my Body Talk practitioner would say I'd done a very good job with: being emotionally strong. But she wondered if he too was as emotionally deep, with strong and powerful energy who understood how the world and universe worked as I did. Ashley suggested that possibly I never taught

Scott how to control and express his real emotions and they just came out as anger because he had never seen me cry; all he ever saw was my strength. "Maybe he is experimenting on you to understand and learn how to express his own emotions" she said. I had never considered that. I had always made sure my son didn't ever feel like he needed to take on a masculine role in the home, so I make sure I was tough. To show him toughness and to let him still be a child without having to put himself in a parental role since I was a single parent. Now, he was almost nine years old and it was worth a try in teaching him in how to manage his emotions. I had spent so much of my time teaching him how to pretend to show emotion it never dawned on me that he did have emotions they were just so deep they would need more help to come out.

Okay. Therefore, I decided next time something like that happened, I would show him, I was sad and I would cry if I needed to. That moment came a month later when the hot water tank broke down and started leaking; the entire basement flooded. I was alone as being the only adult in the home to fix things, and had no idea what to do. I didn't even know how to shut off the main water valve. Scott was right there. So, I cried. He looked at me, shocked and said, "Mom, I have never seen you cry."

I responded, "Yes, I am sad. I don't know how to fix this or even who to call right now. All I need is a hug and then I can figure out my next steps."

He hugged me for a long time. Then I said, "Okay, I am better now. Sometimes crying helps." Then I called my brother-in-law and stepdad to help me. I had someone coming to turn the water off and fix the problem.

Scott had already started cleaning up the mess with towels.

"Its okay, Mom," he said, "we are a family and we will all help clean this up. We'll be fine."

He was right, we would be fine. I knew we would be fine and he had no idea I had set him up to experience this moment with me. His response was amazing and, from then on, he never intentionally caused me any physical harm just to see what my reaction would be. We were still learning together, but we were moving forward. He was teaching me, I was teaching him, and we were growing together.

CHAPTER 30

A KNOWING

I NOW SAW MY son through a completely different lens. Scott struggled with relationships with the majority of men. They would have a difficult time being in the same space with Scott while still understanding him. I couldn't blame them, it was frustrating, I knew that. Scott would ask questions non-stop and refuse to follow directions. It appeared to be a sign of disrespect, and the men in my life couldn't tolerate that. They expected kids to listen and fall in line, to do what they are told. Not my son.

Scott was old enough now that Jack and him are now developing an amazing relationship. Scott shared with me that he can't talk to anyone else but me; he still shares his nightmares, stories, worries, secrets and concerns with me when he comes back from visiting anyone. He knows I understand how he thinks.

I decided to move closer to Scott's father so they could nurture their relationship. Before we moved, we needed renovations done on our home. Erin's dad, Ralph, came to do them. After two days at our place, Ralph told me he found Scott to be a boy like none other he had met before. He said he was the kindest soul for such a young child and that he thought Scott was special. They really seemed to love each other, to the point where Scott went right to Ralph the second he got home from school, and he always wanted Ralph to eat with us. Ralph filled our home with such a masculine presence of love that I had never felt before. He saw Scott the way no one else but I did.

Months after we'd moved into our new home, Scott asked me, "Mom, who do I live with if you and Dad both die?"

I told him that we have tons of family and that *if* anything like that were to ever happen, he would be with his family. I paused and then asked him, "Who, out of your family, would you want to live with if that happened?"

"Ralph, Mom. I would want to live with Ralph. He knows me."

I teared up. I have tons of family that we see often; so does his father. Children know when they are truly loved for being themselves. Scott knew that Ralph truly cared about him. I felt privileged to have an amazing best friend like Erin, and grateful that she had brought her father into my son's life as well. I'm not sure how I could have gotten through this all without Erin. They are our chosen family—our soul family.

I realized that talking more and more with Scotty was showing me how he saw the world. I decided I would set aside time just for him and I to talk about the world and spirituality. I didn't know how to open up the conversation until the moment presented itself.

One day, when we were driving, Scott said, "Mom, do you remember that day when you killed animals?"

Shocked by his comment, I explored more. "What are you talking about?"

He responded, "Remember, you killed a duck, a deer and a bird."

A Knowing

I realized he was talking about the animals I'd hit while driving. he looked at everything as if it were intentional. I thought about it for a long time.

I replied." Well, those are called accidents Scott. I didn't mean to kill them with my vehicle. I wish I didn't kill them, but we didn't have enough time to save them without driving off the road."

"I would have rather died though then have those animals die Mom." He said

My son, who had harmed animals in the past was now saying he would die for an animal. Nothing was lining up, which meant I needed to ask more questions. "Why would you want to die instead of the animal?"

"Because when we die we just come back as something else mom, so dying isn't a bad thing. We all die mom."

"Wow Scott, well you're right we all die and the idea that we all come back as something else is called reincarnation." *Maybe, this whole time, his curiosity about death and animals has been because he knows there is life after death, but is too young to process it?*

I told him I agreed with his theory. I said, "I believe in energy and that we are all connected by it; it flows around us and within us."

"That's right mom and I would kill for an animal because they don't hurt anyone like people do and we don't actually die when we die." I paused in disbelief that my son was so profound in what he was saying. So, I decided to sit in the space of understanding his perspective. I chose to be his student; he was my spiritual teacher. After all, do we really know? Maybe children who struggle with life today truly understand our connectedness to all things.

Scott said, "Yanno mom, my energy that flows inside of

me is the colour red. I don't know why its red, but that's what colour it is. There is also a small part of it that is dark red. I'm afraid of that dark red colour mom."

Blown away, I pressed on. "Well, Scott, I think that there is balance in everything. I think that dark and light colours of all kinds have to exist together. So, I wouldn't be afraid of the dark red colour or the darkness as long as you try to understand it and see how it can help you grow. As long as your light red colour was the majority of your energy, you will be okay and in charge of your darkness that way."

"Hmmm" He thought. "My dark red colour is only in the right side of my leg mom and I feel like I can control it now."

A smile drew across my face infatuated with the boy I was having this conversation with. I have never been so proud. I was proud that he was mine to teach and learn from on this journey of life together. "I love your brain Scott, I always have and I love the way you think."

"I know mom, I love you too and I love animals too mom."

From then on, there were more and more stories that expressed the level of his compassion. We were no longer playing a game or fighting with each other for control or a sense of winning. We had moved on from playing chess against each other and we were now playing chess against the world. We were now searching, learning, moving and growing together. Now I was able to witness his beautiful soul through loving eyes. He taught me life isn't a game… it's a journey.

CHAPTER 31

SAVIOUR

FOR SCOTT'S EIGHTH birthday party, we had eight of his friends at our house. Scott showed the kids my singing bowls. Right after he played the bowls for the boys, the energy in the home elevated to the point where one of the boys said he needed to go home and couldn't handle being there. He had to stay in a closet by himself while we waited for his mother. And then all of sudden the energy shifted into something I have never seen from a group of young boys.

Scott started to cry "Mom, this is the worst birthday ever since Lyle has to leave."

Ryan instantly started to cry, "Scott, I have never seen you cry and it makes me cry. I am so sad too."

Derek said to his twin brother Jason "Jason, lets go an protect Lyle outside of the closet so that we can show him we will protect him." Derek was crying grabbing his gun and so was Jason.

Paul started hysterically crying on the couch "This is the worst birthday ever!" He would scream. "I can't believe Scott is crying, I have never seen Scott cry."

Scott responds while still crying "Its because I am in my home and I am the most comfortable in my home and can cry here. There are lots of things to cry for."

Paul responded, "I know Scott, like when I miss my dad when he is gone it makes me cry."

From the bedroom, you could hear Derek say, "When my dad went to jail it made me really sad and I cried a lot too."

I couldn't believe my ears that all of these boys were crying and talking about how they cry about real hard things in life. Lyle's mom got there and he went home.

I said. "Ok boys we are all going to go to Scott's room and sit on the bed in a circle. Let's talk about our sadness."

Jason replied still crying, "I am so sad that Lyle left and it makes me sad about my dad."

We all went to the bedroom and the boys wept and wept and wept. There was no sharing at that point, but all of the boys cried and hugged. It was beautiful. When everyone felt their tears were done we left the room and went back to birthday nerf gunfights and cake.

A fun birthday party turned into a sharing and hug circle for a group of boys ready to talk. My son had just helped his friends process some deep emotional trauma. He had played the bowls for his friends and shown them how to cry. He was a leader, a healer. I needed to be more observant and talk to him more about how he sees and feels about the world. I have learned that he has a huge sense of compassion for others.

We had recently moved from a small town to a large city. Scott talked about how he didn't understand why there are homeless people. He wanted to take them home with us, or give them money. When I explained mental illness and residential schools, he said, "Who thought that would be a good idea? That was dumb, you don't treat people like that." My son, whom I once thought would harm others, was an advocate for the most vulnerable people.

Since my son was young, he has always been attracted to wolves. I went on a week-long self-care retreat where I had a vision of myself as an elk. It felt so powerful and strong, it made me weep. I felt such gratitude for this beautiful animal. Shortly thereafter, I searched for the meaning behind the elk. Was this my spirit animal or an animal sending me a message? I came across a first nations' story about the wolf and the elk.

Before the wolf existed, man hunted the elk for food and other essentials. The most desirable of all the elk were the bigger, stronger ones. They would have an abundance of meat on them and produce larger pelts. Soon enough, the only elk left to hunt were the weaker ones. Man would soon starve. The creator knew he needed to produce an animal that would chase and eat the weak elk so the stronger elk could continue to reproduce stronger offspring to provide food for the nation. That's when the wolf was introduced to the Earth—to kill the weaker elk.

Overwhelmed with emotion, that's when I realized my son was my wolf. Without him, I would not be the pillar of strength I am today. I was filled with gratitude that my son had chosen me as his mother.

He's also an amazing big brother. One day, I walked in while he was pretending to play a video game with his sister. It appeared she was winning but the TV wasn't even working. Scott had put on a YouTube video of racing and was cheering her on. That's who my son truly is— my hero, my wolf. We are no longer playing the game of chess. I also came to realize out of the people he will be here to help, he came to help me the most.

CHAPTER 32

ADAPTING

THINGS WERE MOVING along so nicely, but I had become so focused on the spiritual and energetic part of his growth that I forgot there needs to be balance on the scientific and medical side as well. So, when Scott stole a toy from the store I was devastated again since we had made such large gains with meditation. The day I found a toy in his pocket while shopping I gave him and X for stealing. Even though, I knew how to handle the consequence I felt like we were now working backwards. I had to stop my thinking and remind myself that it's a combination and that the balance is key. I just kept plugging away at my ticks and tokens program and it wasn't until my appointment with the pediatrician that I discovered he was probably stealing and lying because his ADHD wasn't properly medicated. The doctor put Scott on baby doses of Intuniv and Biphenten and ... "poof" no more stealing and lying. I realized that when any behavior came up I needed to assess it first to decide which avenue to look at it from.

When he started in a new school, he couldn't understand the after-school program coordinator, there was a language barrier. Every single day the after-school manager would talk to me about how Scott doesn't respect other children's boundaries or follow the rules. I gave Scott two X's in a row for being talked to by the school program. On the second day it was over Scott not wearing snow pants when asked to put them on. I thought it was very minor, but I told Scott whenever the school talked to me it would be an X. He had not been on a level five for years and now I would have to take away his technology for an entire week. When Scott lost privileges, he lost hope in everything. I couldn't let years of success go backward, but I could NOT give him yet another X. So, while I was talking to the after school program manager about the snow pants, Scott ran away. I could tell by the way the manager was talking to me that he didn't like Scotty yet. So, I told the manager he would get an X and then I went looking for Scott. When I found Scott, he was hiding because he was upset, knowing what the consequence would be. He didn't want to be on level five. I decided in this moment that I needed to build a fake relationship between him and the manager, so that things didn't get worse. I learned this technique in the attachment course I had taken. I told Scott that I wanted to give him an X BUT his after-school program manager told me not too. Scott's face lit up. I stayed mad. I said, "He is the reason you aren't getting one, so you better thank him on our way out."

Scott thanked the coordinator and that was our last X with the after school program. Creating a fake attachment worked. I lied to keep my authority with the program and to create a false connections between two people that did not like each other based on lying about the situation and how it unfolded. The after-school program manager had no idea what I had said to Scott, but thanked me for being consistent with him. It was in that moment that I realized things have been going well for a full year now and Scott melting down again would put me in

Adapting

a vulnerable position, so knowing how he reacted to situations allowed me to know his thought patterns and be ahead of him.

These moments warm my heart because this makes me his biggest fan knowing we have made it so far in a short amount of time. What we are doing is actually working, for both of us, and what I did in that moment…. actually worked. I fall more and more in love with my son every day. He even calls me Bro now, but still respects my authority.

CHAPTER 33

NOW WHAT

I WOULD BE LYING if I said I knew how to handle the next situation with Scott coming at me. It's all trial and error, but I now know how to stay on my toes and two steps ahead of him. Of course, I still have fear about what the teenage years might look like for him. Just the other day, Scott reminded me that he used to bite me. I asked him if he brought it up because he was proud of how he hurt me. He smirked. I am no longer afraid for his future as I am ready for any worst case scenario that presents itself, because I unconditionally love him no matter what. At the end of the day, I can proudly say I tried everything to raise my son into a healthy individual. Every day is still a new challenge, but now I know the game is over. There is a bigger purpose and a place for my son in this world. There are no opponents. We are all made from love and are meant to spread love; he was brought into my life to teach me that. There are so many others like him, here to help us all grow and learn as individuals and a society.

The most important lesson I have learned is that it takes a slice from every type of health professional, allopathic and "complementary," in order to raise these special children in order to help us fall in love with them and embrace what they are here to do. We should only use labels and diagnoses as forms of knowledge and not equate a person's identity with them. Even an Indigo child has some kind of "diagnosis"—ADHD, ODD, OCD, Anxiety, Sensory Dysregulation, Conduct Disorder, Antisocial Personality Disorder, Psychopath, Autism, Empath, etc.—all labels I have used to help me understand Scott. Then, I rid him of them and fell in love with the complexity of who he is. At the end of the day, he is just Scott, my son. Because I worked hard to rid him of the labels, he will no longer be limited—he can expand far and wide to change this world. Elements of our society don't always work well together, and it takes you as a parent to figure out which slice you need to take from each professional and program for your own child. I have learned to tell the programs and professionals what they want to hear because we have not yet moved to a place where we can embrace the missing spiritual component of being human, but I have faith mind, body and soul approaches to having a child with a label will someday be embraced by the masses. Until then, remember, you're important too, take care of yourself, so trust yourself...... you are not alone.

REFERENCE LIST

Attachment/Trauma Expert:

Tracy Cook A., M.Sc., RSW, CCTP, DDP; Cook Counselling Services Ltd. Connection Intensive Treatment Homes. Edmonton, Alberta Canada http://www.cookcounselling.com/

Autism/Behavioural Specialist:

Erin Gluckie: Behavioural Analyst, MB-ABA, BCBA, Edmonton Alberta Canada. https://www.linkedin.com/in/erin-gluckie

Asperger's Resource/Autism Level One:

https://www.aspergerexperts.com/, online resource.

BodyTalk Practitioners:

Allison Bachmeier, Body Talk Practitioner; BodyTalk Instructor, Vibrant Transformation https://vibranttransformation.com/

Ashely Rowland-Moellenbeck, BodyTalk Practitioner, Soul Movement, Canada. https://www.facebook.com/pages/category/Alternative-Holistic-Health-Service/Soul-Movement-447073599405836/

Empath Oil:

Kim Wuirch, Author, Spiritual Mentor, Psychic Healer and Empath, Employed by Angels. kimwuirch.com

Indigo:

Wikipedia: The free encyclopedia. (2004, July 22). FL: Wikimedia Foundation, Inc. Retrieved August 10, 2004, from https://en.wikipedia.org/wiki/Indigo_children

Meditation Link:

New Horizon guided meditation for children. https://www.youtube.com/user/NewHorizonHolistic

www.ingramcontent.com/pod-product-compliance
Lightning Source LLC
Chambersburg PA
CBHW030909080526
44589CB00010B/215